The Spirit Intercedes

The Spirit Intercedes

The New Testament in Prayers and Images

K. K. Yeo

with illustrations by

S. Claire Matheny

CASCADE *Books* • Eugene, Oregon

THE SPIRIT INTERCEDES
The New Testament in Prayers and Images

Cascade Books
A Division of Wipf and Stock Publishers
199 W. 8th Ave., Suite 3
Eugene, OR 97401

www.wipfandstock.com

ISBN 13: 978-1-60608-794-7

Cataloging-in-Publication data:

Yeo, Khiok-Khng.

The Spirit intercedes : the New Testament in prayers and images / K. K. Yeo ; illustrations by S. Claire Matheny.

ISBN 13: 978-1-60608-794-7

xvi + 116 p. ; 23 cm.

1. Prayers. 2. Bible. N.T. —Illustrations. 3. Christian art and symbolism. 4. Aesthetics—Religious aspects—Christianity. I. Matheny, S. Claire. II. Title.

BV245 Y46 2009

Manufactured in the U.S.A.

Contents

Images

All illustrations in this book are available in color from the following website:

http://kkyeo.com/

Preface

Order and Mystery

DESIRING GOD

IN THE FIRST EIGHTEEN years of my atheist life, I (K. K.) longed for "someone out there" to whom I could express my innermost desire, joy, and pain. Gradually in my theological search I came to believe that the universe has its Creator, that life possesses order and purpose, and that we are not alone. Becoming a Christian was such a dramatic event in my life; I find that now I can commune with a transcendental Being who cares for his creatures personally. I can also flourish as a member of the body of Christ.

Upon my Christian conversion, I was content to pray simply—my thoughts similar to baby talk. I learned in early youth, however, that prayers express my desire to know God rather than my desire simply to grasp God's gifts. "O God, you are my God, I seek you, my soul thirsts for you; my flesh faints for you" (Ps 63:1). Prayers of young Christians are often innocent in motive and pure in heart.

In my adult years, I struggle to maintain a childlike mystery. I have found that neither Christian life nor theology has the absolute power to make sense of God's actions in the world. Prayer does not lead me to a laundry list—matching God's will with events—personal, social, national, or cosmic. Instead, through public and private prayers I seek communion with my Creator. They paint the relationship I have with God, in the mountaintop and the valley-of-death moments, or more frequently, in the dull and ordinary rhythm of my days. Because prayers for me are akin to two lovers living and getting along together, I often rejoice in the fact that prayer transcends rhetoric and reveals the attitude and intention of my heart. Prayer represents the ceaseless posturing of the created before the Creator, our eternal Life Partner. Prayer relies on our aesthetic moments—those artistically articulated or groaned by the Spirit. Through our intimacy with scripture, we find that our human stories are embraced by God's story. Though we cannot name, explain, or always understand life events, we identify ourselves as God's children with spoken and unspoken prayer as our deepest form of divine communication.

PRAYING WITH WORDS AND PICTURES

I love teaching because I learn so much. As a New Testament professor, I often comment to students that studying the Bible academically provides only a foretaste of theological and spiritual understanding. As much as I believe that we learn from biblical figures and narratives what it means to be a child and servant of God, I encourage students to allow the biblical texts to baptize them. The life of faith requires an immersion into Bible reading, research, and meditation until a believer's thoughts and speech are conditioned by the living Word. The collection of prayers in this volume illuminate my pedagogical purpose. A familiarity with the text depends not solely on the science of biblical research, but most crucially, on one's desire to know God intimately through the scripture.

Here, among my written prayers are the drawings of Claire Matheny. They echo the sentiments of my language, but also take on a life of their own—combining her own faith experience and knowledge of Scripture in artistic expression. Our textual and visual prayers uplifted together provide a fuller picture of biblical imagery than either can alone. We seek to channel God's creative energy by praying and painting for what is impossible and possible, what is inspiring and uninspiring, what is beautiful or shameful, what is hopeful or meaningless, what is joyful or painful.

Artful Prayers and Prayerful Poesis

Prayer is the means whereby God's image in us is restored, as God's presence transforms us from one degree of glory to another (2 Cor 3:18); our desire is for the prayers and drawings to serve as a mirror, able to reflect the glory of God on human beings. "To be human" in the best sense of the phrase is to reject sinfulness as part of our humanity and to recognize the glory and beauty and virtue God originally creates in and through us. In our humanness, we also learn to accept our weaknesses (need of food and rest, for example), struggles (with trial and temptation), and limitations (of space and time). Paintings and prayers are the means of not simply our confession of sins, but also the stations of rest/peace with God. Through paintings and prayers, of course, we know how we draw strength and wisdom from God as we are created to be in the world (limitation and self-transcendence)—enabling us to be at one with ourselves and with others. Our brushstrokes illustrate both our brokenness and redemption in Christ. Our indwelt divine love inspires prayers that are groaning "too deep for words"

(Rom 8:26). When we pray, we sense divine grace endowed not only to the self, but to the unifying of community. We invite all of you to join us as God's moves through words, figures, and colors.

Those who see the faces and the colors of the Spirit will seek in turn to incarnate God's gifts in Christ to the world. The aesthetic interrelationship between God and humans serves as the basis for poetic justice. Such ethical responsibility of prayer channels God's love and order as justice for the world through his faithful people. Prayers in *poesis,* e.g., paintings, therefore connect us with the depth of God and peoples, and move us to become compassionate beings. As our inner child reminds us, the prayerful movement of a crayon can conform us to the body of Christ. Older now, we turn to written and artful prayer in order to rediscover the most innate movements of the Spirit.

SELF-EMPTYING TOWARDS WHOLENESS

The freedom of expression and painting swings like a pendulum between obedience and liberation. We are created to be born slaves *and* friends of God. To be fully human ourselves is to "forget" and to "deny" ourselves. The *imitatio Christi,* making room for others, constantly undoes the "mimetic violence" (René Girard) of the narcissistic self. The *imitatio Christi* self-denial is not self-hatred, but the responsible self knowing others' welfare as her own. Thus, by assuming responsibility to serve, her own self is restored to the web of life, the beauty of the cosmic life. God's Spirit who is "All and in all" (1 Cor 15:28) requires the prayers to take on a *kenotic* (self-emptying) posture. This similar posture is lived out early on in the old (meaning, proved to be true) scripture as Samuel responded to God, "speak, Lord, your servant is listening" (1 Sam 3:9). In the new (meaning, *novum*, or surprisingly hopeful and potent) scripture, a young woman by the name of Mary uttered the words of Magnificat regarding the miracle of God on her fragile life, "let it be with me according to your word" (Luke 1:38). Everyone who paints prayers or who prays their pictures of God throughout the centuries takes on this humble and expectant posture.

God's wisdom serves as the ultimate *speech (prayer)-act (painting)* that portrays our authentic self. Not our impulses or designs, but God's eternal life and precepts are the source of self-offering love. Thus, to pray is to surrender oneself (yet in turn find one's full self). The "I" or the "we" who prays presumes that God is the Subject rather than the Object, and that God will enlighten our voice and passion in Christ. The Divine Subject empowers human subjects to experience the real presence and glory of God. Prayers then represent an intersubjective reflection on creation—joyous and lamenting, dependent, and yet, enabling the soaring of the eagle's wings (Isa 40:31). The self is not its own origin, but serves instead as a mouthpiece of God's original love for creation.

Prayers and paintings reveal paths to cultivate the aesthetic delight of the mysterious yet intimate relationship one has with God. In that relationship, nothing is fixed. The world in God's view is transparent, fluid, and open. Therefore, the more open one is with God in prayer, the more candidly one prays, and the more intimately one connects to the Source of all creation. Our attempt here is not to express or paint the mystery of godly relationship away. Prayer and painting draw us to the light, but the pilgrimage is often intensified by silence and groaning. Prayer is not a magical formula, it is a life animated by the Spirit of God who manifests divine grace. Prayer is not buying insurance, it is not asking for a precise roadmap. Prayer shows directions circling God's throne and human brokenness. A foretaste of God's goodness and beauty and truth for the cosmos is enough to court us in prayer even as we are lost to despair: "Bless the Lord, O my soul, and all that is within me, bless his holy name" (Psa 103:1).

Life-long Learners of the Word and the Spirit

As a seminary graduate, I (Claire) launch into pastoral ministry with theological questions that often only find resonance for me through art. I discover that the "colors and faces of the Spirit" are revealed—not only as we encounter the biblical text, but also as we learn to give expression to our own longings. Each artistic piece brings me to a fresh encounter with God's mystery, as well as reawakens me to my own self-limitations. Our prayerful offerings combined represent the efforts of a teacher and a student, of two individuals on their own journeys of faith. However, I believe that if we seek to live "in Christ," we cannot help but impact each other in every intentional word offered in prayer. We cannot help but be blessed by the images that illustrate our human longing. We pray because we wish, even in the weak moments of our disobedience, to be in more deep relationship with our sovereign God and the glory of creation. After all, we are life-long learners of the Word, the Spirit, Life itself.

We hope the prayers and the paintings in this collection will help readers to trust God more, allowing the Wholly Other to shine his light and grace and mercy upon us, and therefore enabling us all to live with thanksgiving and with "peace that surpasses all understanding" (Phil 4:7).

K. K. Yeo and Claire Matheny
Epiphany, 2009

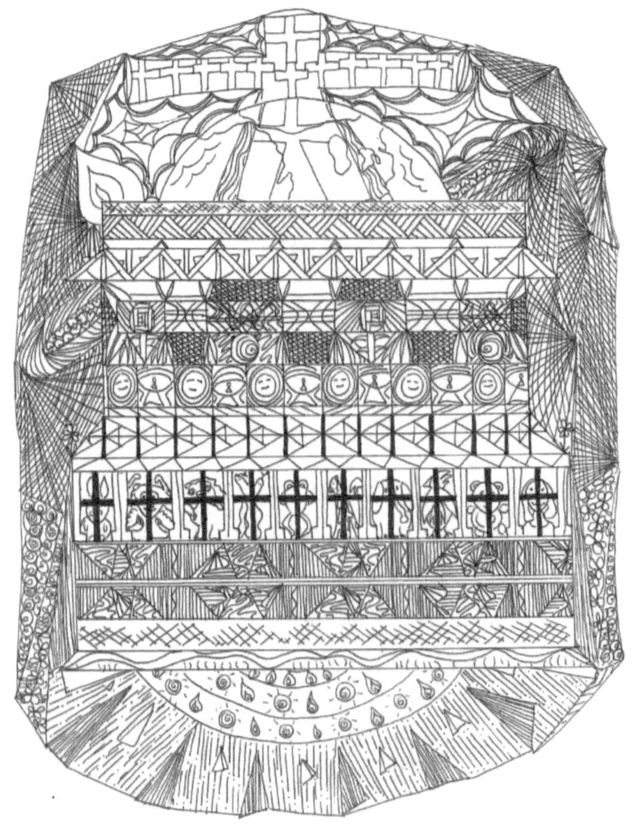

Order and mystery

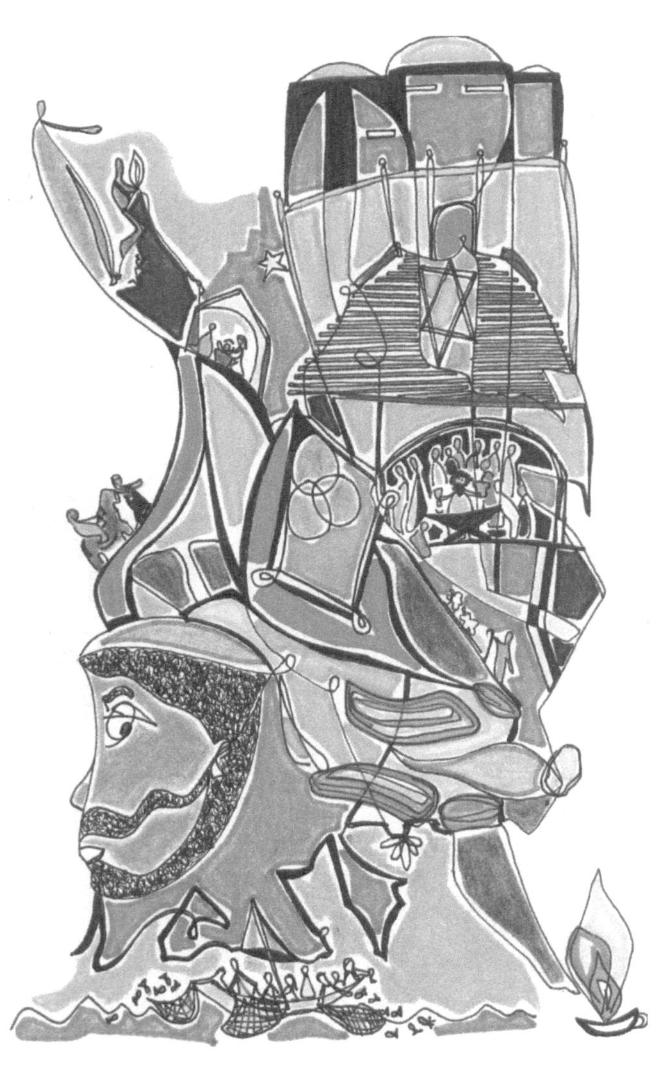

Baptized. Tempted. Broken.
The gospel unveils the Risen Lord

1

Promise of the Old and Hope of the New (Matthew)

God of Abraham and Sarah,
    show us today your faithfulness and mercy.
Imprint upon us the life of your beloved Son,
    for Abel who was slain speaks, Isaac who was bound is
        set free.

God of Moses and Miriam,
    speak to us the promise of the old and the hope of the
        new.
Instill in us the spirit of your wisdom
    that we might fulfill the past and remember the future.

God of Rahab, Ruth and David,
    fill us with your love that never gives us up.
Transform our sins and suffering into joy filled service,
    conform our will to do the work of mercy,
    reform our desire to forgive others and treat them
        as your own.
Energize us to bear the yoke of your Torah,
    the law that showers upon us freedom to love you and
        our neighbors.

God of Mary and Joseph,
grant us calmness of heart to trust in your Spirit,
for you come visiting us with surprises,
and indwelling us with ever renewing life.
Emmanuel, when we are insecure and lost,
grant us shalom in you.

God of Jesus,
have mercy on us when we wear the masks of hypocrites and cynic;
kindle in our hearts the passion for you and your church,
even though the church sometimes hurts us.
Forgive us that we might forgive,
discipline us to know your beloved Son that we might be your children.
Train us to proclaim the gospel of our Master,
whose coming brings us your blessing and your peace,
in Christ's name, we pray. Amen!

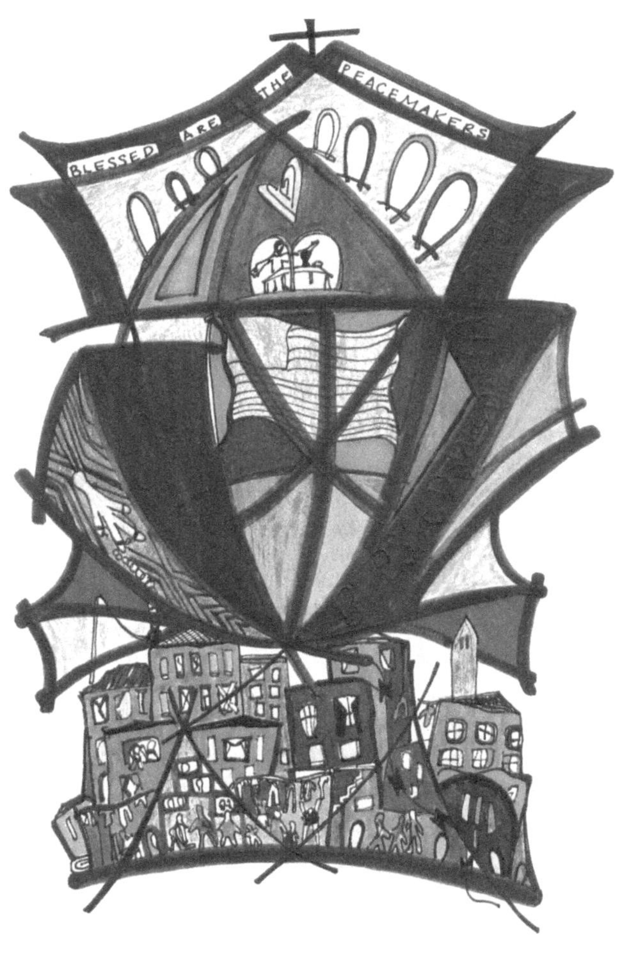

In all places
God, in our cities, in our hearts, we desire your shalom!

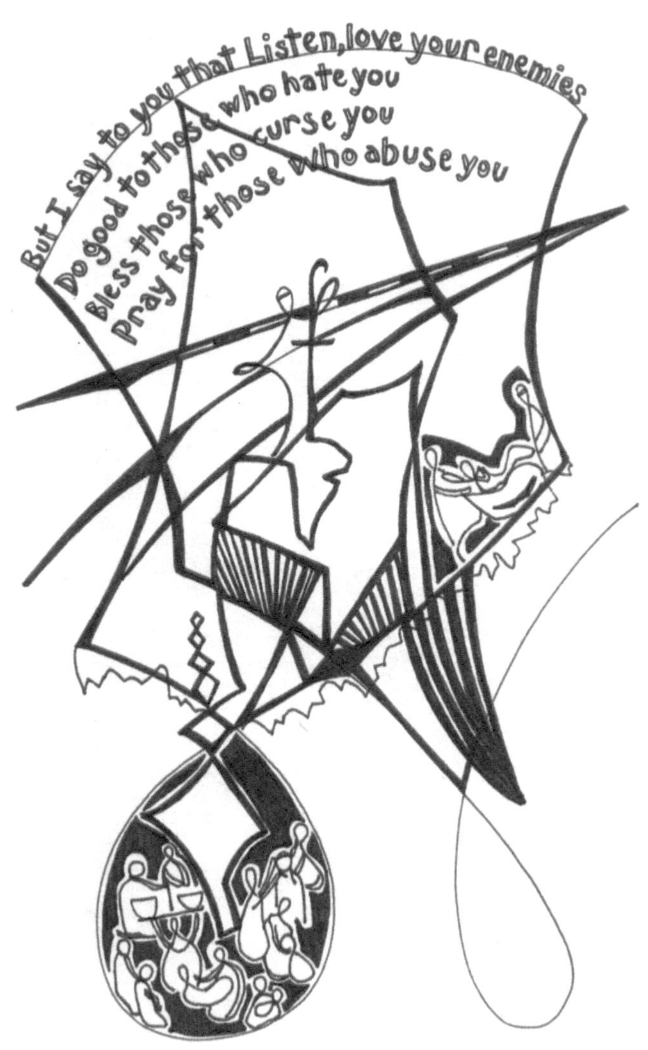

But I say to you

2

Have Mercy on Us[1] (Matthew 5)

Gracious God,
have mercy on us when the freedom of our country
defines the Christian utopia,
when our market economy defines the ultimate hope,
make us poor in spirit that we might be rich in your
kingdom.
Have mercy on us when the love of our country becomes
our religion,
when our American dream becomes others' nightmare,
when our comfort becomes others' burden,
and our security becomes others' bondage,
help us to repent and mourn so that we might be
comforted.
Have mercy on us when military power becomes our
domination,
teach us to be meek thus inheriting the shalom of the
world.

1. Written on September 11, 2001, as an American Christian, to reflect on his responsibilities as a world Christian.

Bestow the blessings that come when we seek your
righteousness,
for only your justice can satisfy our hunger,
your love can quench our thirst.
Forbid us to be merciless,
forbid us to conquer and retaliate in your name.
When we think of Washington D. C., and Riyadh, Jerusalem,
help us see the tears of Christ.

Make our hearts pure in thinking of you,
simple in obeying you,
one in trusting you.
When we are in fear and despair,
be with us, Emmanuel,
that we might see a glimpse of your glory!
When we are insecure,
assure us that you have accepted us as your beloved.
Yes, Lord, "Blessed are the peacemakers,
for they will be called children of God."

Give us the vision of your reign,
the rule of your righteousness,
grant us confidence in you and courage to proclaim
your kingdom;
for the sake of Christ, Amen!

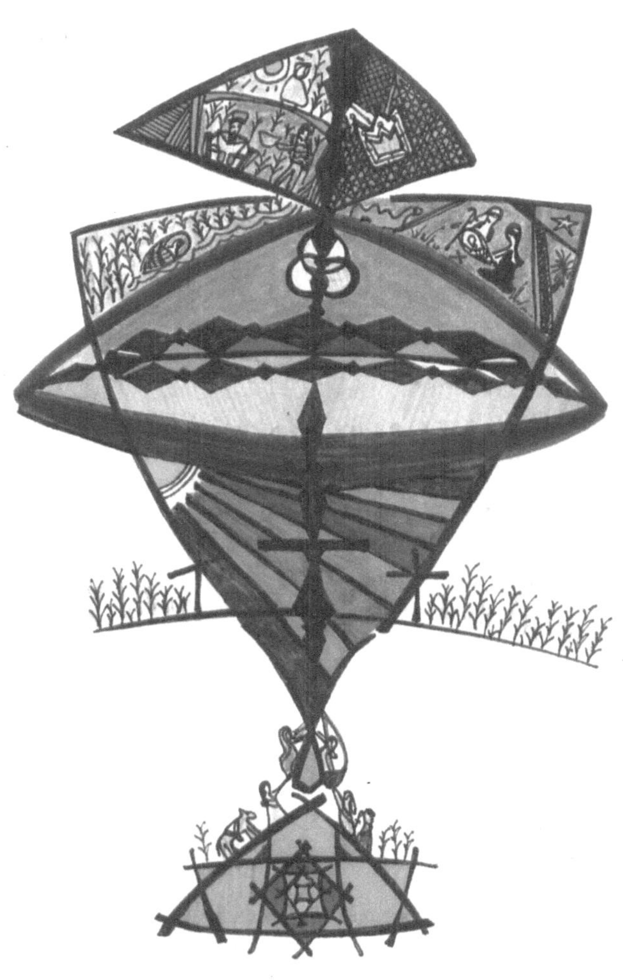

Resting in your chalice

3

Finding Rest in Your Yoke (Matthew 11)

"Come to me, all you that are weary and are carrying heaven burdens, and I will give you rest. Take my yoke upon you, and learn from me; for I am gentle and humble in heart, and you will find rest for your souls. For my yoke is easy, my burden light." (11:28–30)

Gracious God,
forgive us so often doubting that you are the Messiah,
disbelieving you are in wisdom incarnate in our midst.
Forgive us for failing to recognize the wonders of Elijah and Elisha that the blind receive their sight, the lame walk, the lepers cleansed,
the deaf hear, the dead raised, the poor receive the good news.
Forgive us for worrying too much about boundaries—
ethical or religious—that turn us cold toward you and one another.
Forgive us for hearing the flute music but not dancing,
for hearing cries of this broken world and not knowing how to mourn.

We thank you, Lord of heaven and earth,
    that you have revealed yourself even to infants.
We pray that our intelligence and our studies will not bind us
    but that we may be tempered with a child-like faith
        touched by your Spirit,
        and conditioned in your mercy.
We come to you now weary;
    some carrying heavy burdens.
    Grant us rest, Prince of Peace.

When our hearts are disturbed like the raging sea,
    when we struggle with sins and temptations,
    grant us peace and strength in Christ,
    teach us to trust in your salvation, God of shalom.
When our minds are like stormy weather,
    when we hold grudges against our enemies,
    grant us assurance in Christ that "all is well,"
    and shape us to imitate Christ's humility and gentleness,
God of forgiveness and forgetfulness,
    when our visions are clouded with greed and gain,
    open our eyes that we may behold your glory and
        mercy,
    as the Crucified Messiah shows us.

Train us to be students of your kingdom,
    help us to carry the yoke of the law,
    and learn from Jesus,
    for he is gentle and humble.
Grant us joy and confidence, Holy One of Israel,
    that we might love you and serve our neighbors,
    in Christ's name we pray. Amen!

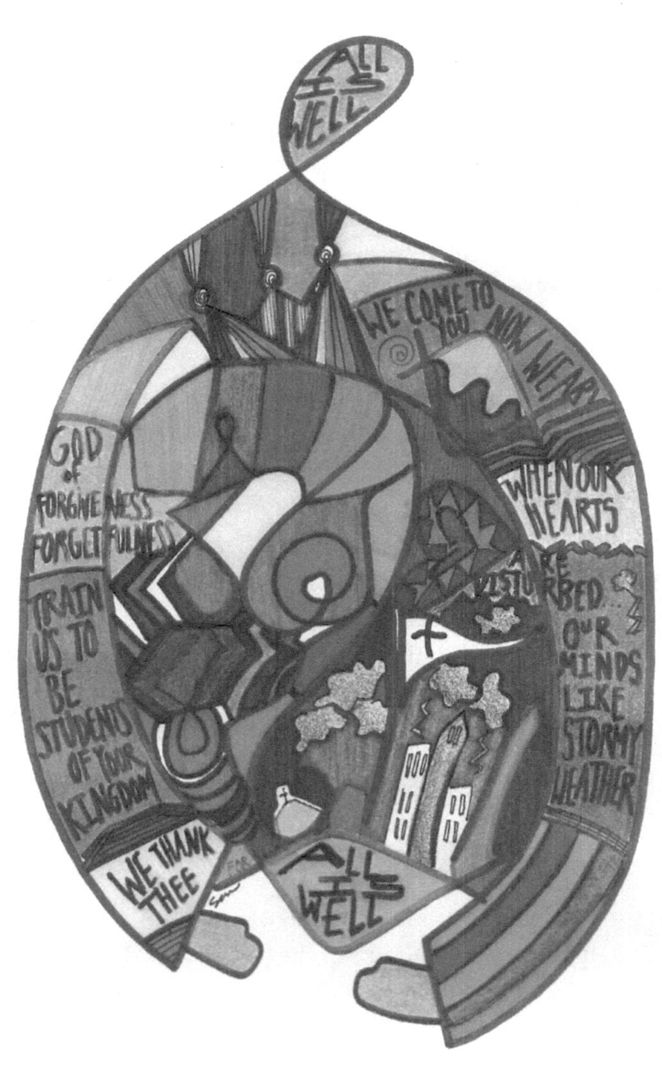

It is well with my soul

4

Our Prayer to the Lord
(Matthew 6:9–13)

Gracious God,
when we pray "our Father in heaven"
make known to us that we are your children,
for your sovereign presence always
surrounds us.
When we pray "hallowed be your name,"
awaken us to know your creation displays your
beauty and glory,
for we are the bearers of your holy.
When we pray "your kingdom come,"
reveal to us the way you reign on all nations and
communities,
and your love and justice rule over all powers and
authorities.
When we pray "your will be done on earth, as it is
heaven,"
teach us to be instruments of your grace
that the lost, the least, and the last will be saved.

We pray that you "give us this day" the bread of the morrow,
for we know the messianic banquet of the Day wipes away our tears of sorrow,
and your love feast creates a community of freedom in the body and blood of Christ.
We pray that you "forgive our sins,"
for we confess that we are sinners saved by grace, sanctified by your Spirit.
We pray that we will "forgive those who wrong us,"
even when we know we are right.
"Lead us not into temptations"
of mediocrity, hatred, and unbelief;
"Deliver us from evils"
of violence, destruction, hopelessness, and apathy.

For all glory and honor and power be yours,
in Christ's name, Amen!

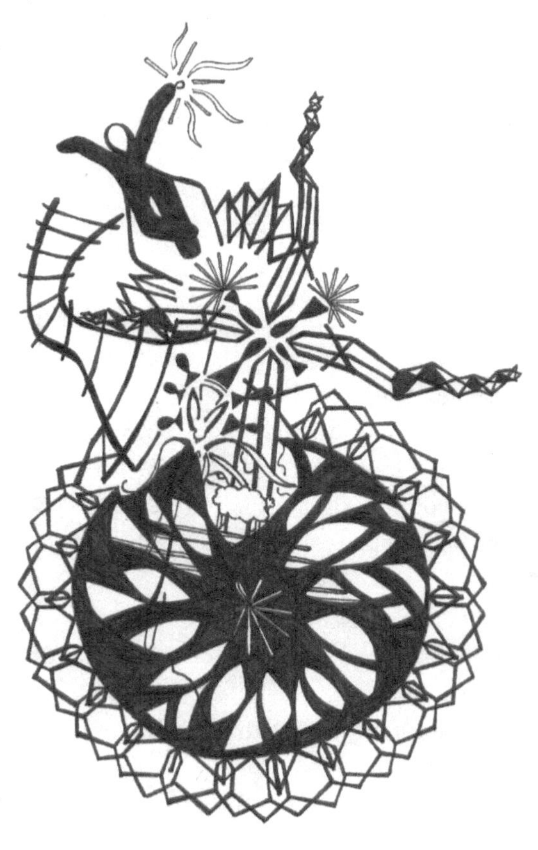

Jagged ladder
Of the world, of God
Jesus Christ
humbled, raised

5

The Son of God Who Died and Served (Mark)

Forgive us, O Lord Jesus,
that we as your disciples are often slow to recognize who you are.
In sickness and death,
we want you to be a healer and a magician;
in fear and disaster,
we want you to be miracle performer and a god who can fix all problems.

Have mercy on us, God of Jesus,
when we want you to meet our convenience and ensure our comfort,
when we exchange our faith in you for your blessings on us,
and when we desire your power to wipe out our enemies.
Instead, the gospel of your Son teaches us
that Jesus' love for you conditioned him to be obedient,
his obedience cost him his life to be ransom for many,
and his trust in you conquers fear and becomes service for all.

Teach us to have eyes of faith,
to behold your glory at the Cross of crucifixion.
Even though we may witness neither miracles nor
resurrection,
yet grant us faith to believe that you are the Son of God.
Show us the destiny of humanity
that your beloved Son demonstrates and leads us to,
that we might thirst for you when we carry our crosses,
in the name of Christ, we pray. Amen!

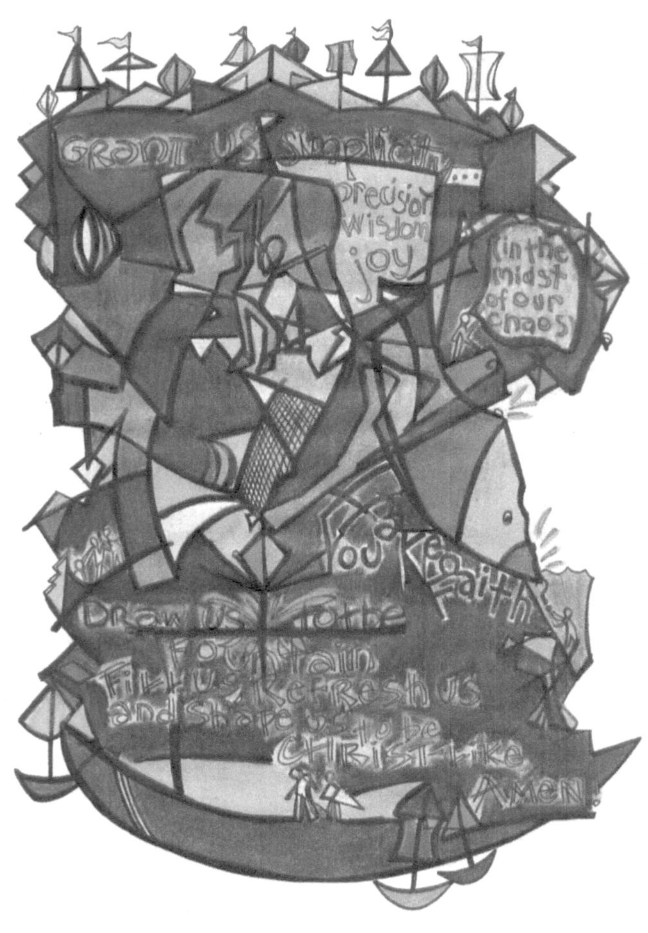

Me. Jonah. Disciples.
Have faith as we fish for peoples

6

Have We No Faith?
(Mark 4:35–41)

Gracious God,
forbid us to live like orphans,
anxious about our comfort and security,
and not knowing our spiritual inheritance.
Forgive us for being your prodigal children,
lost in the cares of the world
and missing your presence.
Be patient with us,
'til we have faith in you;
make us calm to know who you are!
Be gracious to us,
'til we have divine love,
and know what you have already done among us—
the body and the blood of Christ!

Come, Lord Jesus!
Come, even now,
that we might come to you as your beloved children,
and together we feast with you at your table today and 'til that Day.

O Lord Jesus,
you are the food that feeds and satisfies us,
your blood that justifies us,
your body broken, that sanctifies us.
Grant us simplicity of eyes to behold the beauty of your Word,
the precision of mind to know your truth,
the wisdom to accept the salvation of your gospel,
the humility to acknowledge the power of your grace,
the joy of obedience in walking in your law,
so that life abundant will be our inheritance from you.

Come, Holy Spirit, draw us to the fountain of your grace,
the throne of your mercy,
the Cross of your love,
so that life eternal will fill us,
refresh us,
and shape us to be Christ-like, Amen!

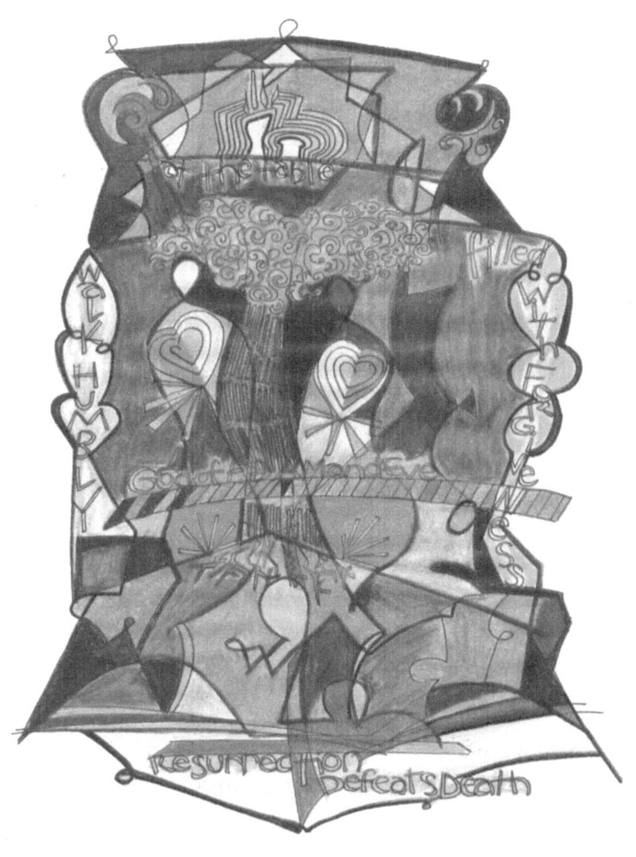

Transform yesterday and today
from the platform of our sin
to the table of your mercy

7

Savior of the World
(Luke)

God of Adam and Eve,
    manifest to us today the image of your Son,
    whose life is the parable of a merciful God—Savior of
        the world.

Shape us as your sons and daughters of God
    to rejoice in your Spirit,
    to remain in prayer,
    to be in kindred spirit
        with the poor, the oppressed, the outcast.
Discipline us as the disciples of Christ
    to be diligent in studying the narrative of your Messiah,
        that our lives might be so inscribed by it,
        we can then bear witness to his coming
            as the salvation of Israel and the light to
                the nations.
Make us walk humbly with you, God of Love,
    that our journey to Jerusalem and places of conflicts
        might be filled with forgiveness and mercy!

As we break bread at your table and your Word,
open our eyes that we might see Jesus,
enlighten us to see the fulfillment of scriptures in Christ
and in our world,
and from the beginning 'til the end, we worship you
as God,
whose wound of love conquers violence,
whose Cross of resurrection defeats death, and
whose coming provides meaning and hope to all
happenings.
Glory be your name, in your mercy we pray. Amen!

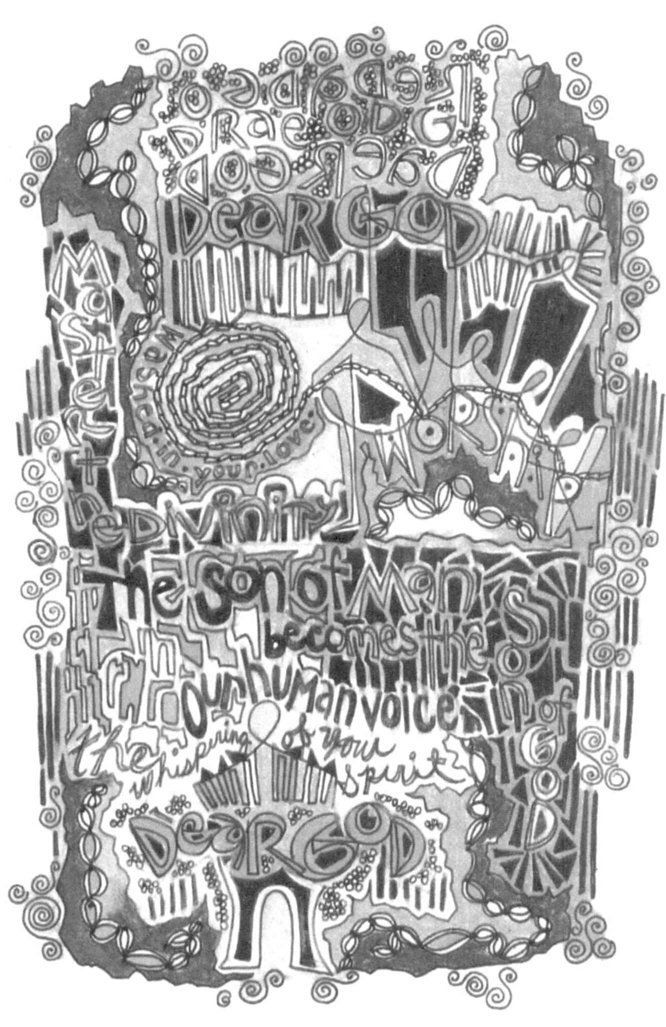

Labyrinth of loss and love
From my will to yours, O God

8

Prodigal Son
(Luke 15)

Dear God,
we love you not because we know how
but because you first love us,
as sinners washed in your love.
We worship you not because we are able
but because you have become one of us,
full of compassion and truth, yet without sins.

Forbid us to love you for our sake
but to love you for the sake of those who are yet to know divine love.
Forbid us to study your Word to master the divinity,
but to study for the benefit of the innocent and the ignorant.
Help us not to worship you as we know how
but to worship you as the parables of Jesus have marveled us,
and illuminating us to return to your mercy seat.

May we not create you an idol of our mind and experience,
but let you create in our mind and experience
the God that shatters all our limits
and assumptions,
'til we bow down before Jesus, and proclaim:
"How great you are!
You are the Son of Man that becomes the Son
of God!"
Human voice, powerful or feeble, will come to an end,
but we pray the whispering of your Spirit
will continue to probe and stir in our hearts,
and the same Spirit who energizes your church in
missions,
'til we worship you in tears and fear.
In the name of your Anointed One, Jeshua, we pray. Amen!

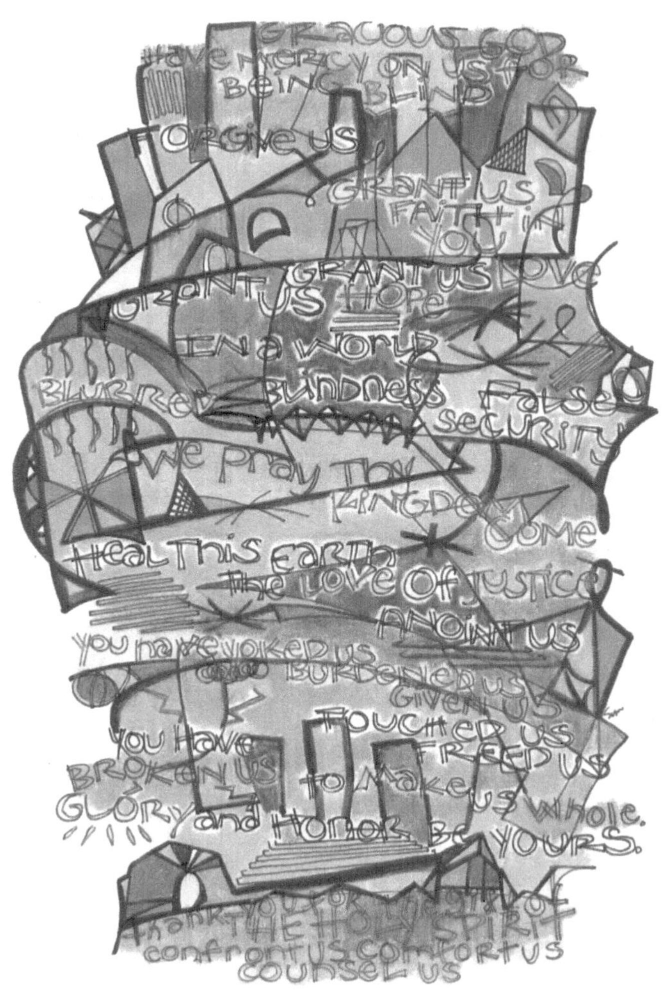

Heal the earth with your justice

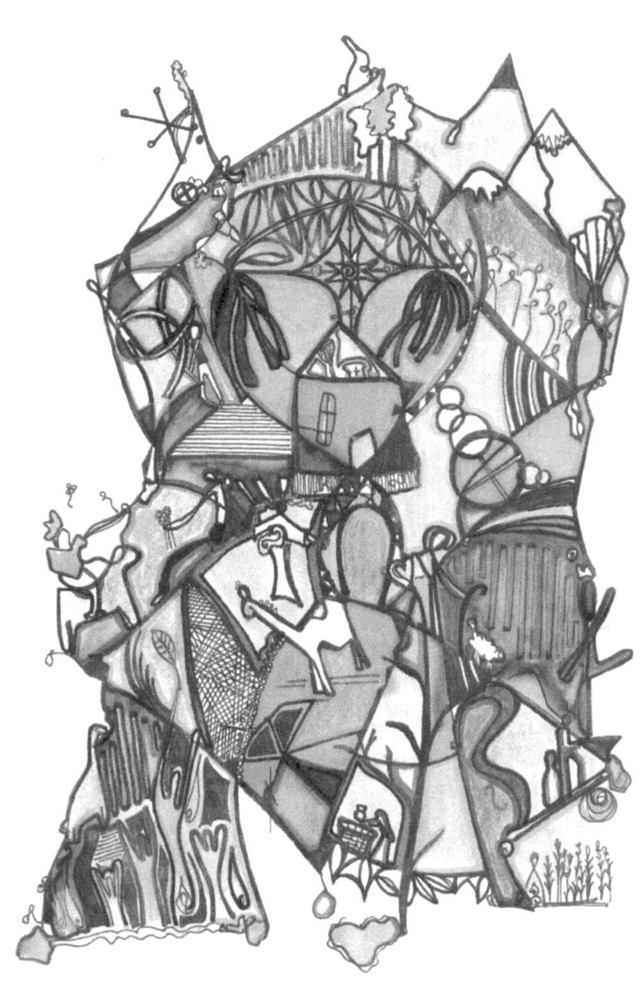

Word made flesh
You liberate creation

9

Logos
(John)

Gracious God,
have mercy on us that we do not see the Sign of
all signs,
for living in linguistic poverty,
unable to scribe your glory.
Forgive us, Lord, for being your servants and knowing
not your joy;
forgive us for being human and yet honor not our
own kind.

Thank you for revealing yourself through your Son
Jesus Christ,
the creative Logos who works miracles and redeems
our sins,
the wisdom Logos who grants life and second chances,
the rhetorical Logos who speaks meaning out of chaos
and destruction.
Grant us faith in you, Christ our Friend,
that we may behold your glory;
grant us love in the community, our Shepherd,
that we may reflect your image;

grant us hope, our Resurrection,
knowing that you are the great I AM,
who is also the Lamb of God,
who stoops down at the lowest point on earth to wash our feet.

In a world of blurred vision and sheer blindness,
help us to behold your image of the invisible God,
the firstborn of all creation, the eternal logos.
In a world of dashed hope and false security,
help us to recognize the glory of God manifest in your sacrificial love.
We pray, your kingdom come, on earth as it is in heaven,
and that your lordship will dethrone idolatrous empires.
May the order of your new creation heal this earth and its diseases.
May the love and justice of your kingdom rule
where wars and injustice and poverty and oppression still dehumanize us.

Anoint us, Spirit of God, to be a people of your good news,
for you have called us to be your friends.
You have yoked us with Christ
that we might break yokes.
You have burdened us with the law
that we might live in the freedom of the command to love.
You have given us sight
that we might bring vision.
You have touched us
to bring healing.

You have freed us
    to bring liberation;
you have broken us
    only to make us whole.
Glory and honor be yours, in Christ's name, Amen!

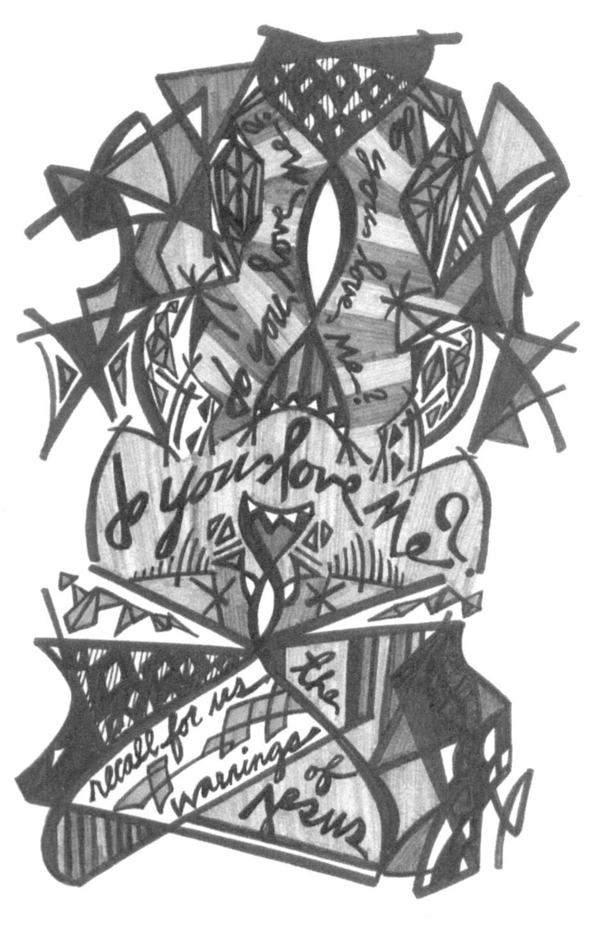

Do we love you?
On our knees
the tears renew us
in worship
in honor

10

Do You Love Me? (John 21)

Gracious God,
    it is proper that we pause in your presence
        for you have tabernacled in our midst, full of grace
            and truth.
    It is right that we worship you before we labor and study
        for you have anointed your beloved Son to be the
            Messiah of the world.
    It is good that we follow you in trust and obedience,
        for Christ, the wounded Savior walks with us the
            path to the Cross of death and resurrection.

When we look at Jerusalem, Chicago, and Pyongyang,
    help us see the tears of Christ!
For in his sorrow is the comfort of the oppressed,
    in his cleansing of the temple the renewal of worship,
    in his suffering the healing of your people.
When we repeatedly do the works of Pharisees, Zealots,
        Sadducees, and the Essenes,
    recall for us the warnings of Jesus.

Our religion will not appease divine wrath,
our force will not overcome differences,
our willpower will not resolve enmity,
our domination will not bring about submission.
Only the peace of Christ will celebrate differences,
his friendship make friends,
his mercy moves us all to joyful obedience.

Teach us to know the language of the scripture,
that we might see the world in your light;
imprint upon us the narrative of your salvation,
that we might serve you with one mind; above all,
baptize us with Christ's passion,
that we might love others as we love you.
Teach us today
to seek your face,
to hear your voice,
to behold your glory, and
to walk in the footsteps of Christ, Amen!

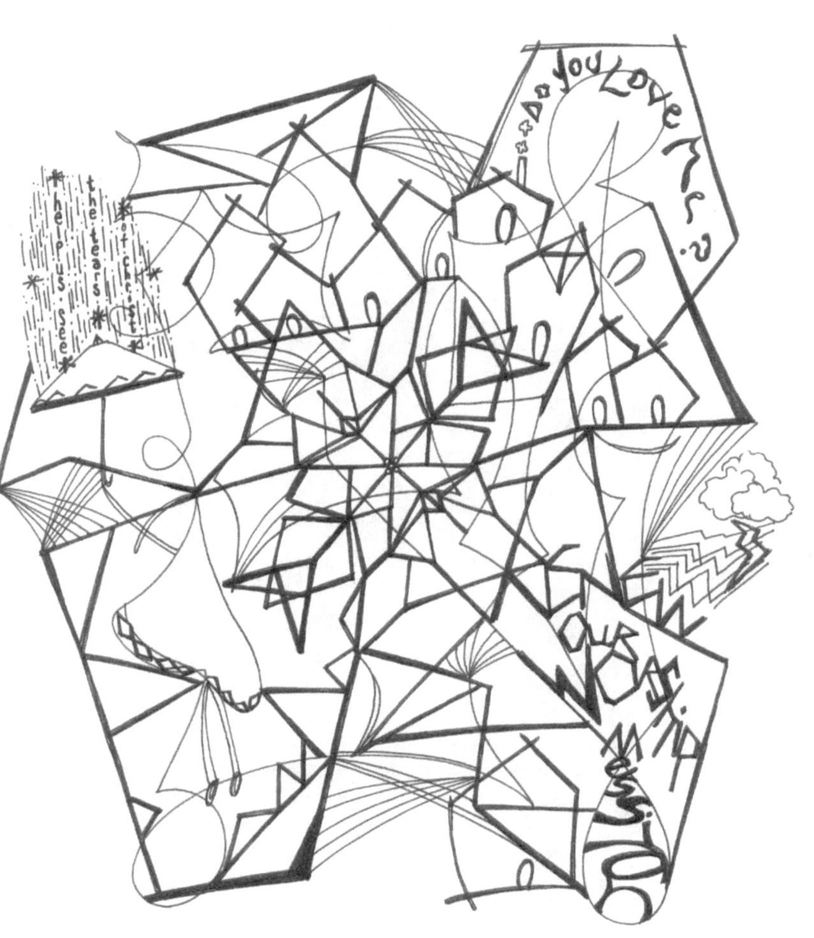

The tears renew us
in praise

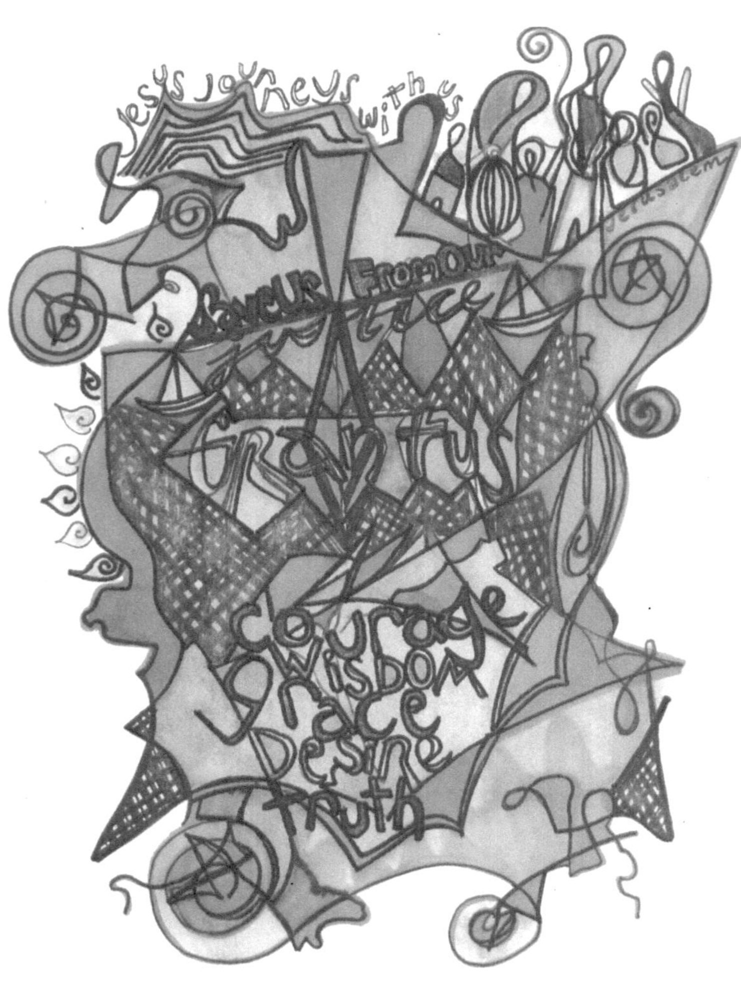

Tongues enflame my tongue

11

Spirit Empowerment Life
(Acts)

Gracious God,
    have mercy on us when our passion for justice
            consumes ourselves;
    when our experience as victim conditions us to be
            suspicious of others
        or to judge them as guilty.
    Have mercy on us when we turn divine justice into
        sibling rivalry;
    when we crucify one another in your name,
        render your gospel powerless to save the world,
        and leave those who need your gospel to die alone
            while your family is torn asunder.

Grant us grace, not as a convenient gift,
    but as your intrusive presence.
Grant us courage, not as an invincible power,
    but as a confident meekness from your Spirit.
Grant us wisdom, not so that we will be clever,
    but so that in humility and trust, we may serve you and
        this community.

Grant us the desire of you rather than of self-interest,
even that of good, of beauty and truth.
For in seeking you and your will alone,
we will please you above all else.
Grant us, truth in discernment,
mercy in justice,
trust in critical reasoning,
wisdom to wholeness.

May the greater good of your kingdom—love—
turn our ethical good into loving mercy.
May the greater truth of your kingdom—faithfulness—
turn our legalistic obedience into thankful service.
May the greater beauty of your kingdom—hope—
turn our utilitarian living into renewal of life.

It is good that we follow you in trust and obedience,
for Jesus journeys with us, the followers, to Jerusalem.
Thank you, Holy Spirit, for you are the divine Gift,
who calls each one of us to fellowship with God
and to be the church engaging in mission.
Thank you, Spirit Divine,
for you confront us, comfort us, counsel us,
energize us to preach the gospel,
to heal the brokenhearted,
to deliver the captives,
to set at liberty those who are bruised,
in Christ's name, Amen!

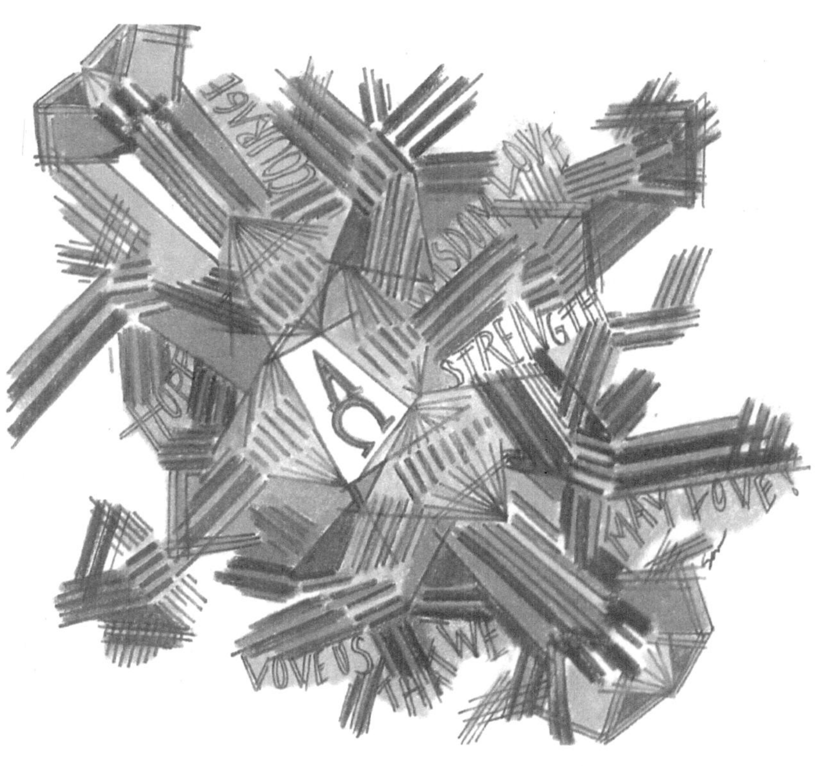

Knowing you, we come to know ourselves

12

God is One (Impartial)
(Romans)

God of Gentiles and Jews,
  barbarians and educated,
  poor and rich,
  south and north,
we worship you for being the Triune God of equality—
  Three in One of unity,
  One in Three of love.

Grant us courage as we seek your face today,
  for it is in knowing you that
  we come to know ourselves.
Grant us wisdom as we seek your voice,
  for it is in hearing your Word
  that we learn to speak the gospel-truth.
Grant us love as we seek your heart,
  for it is by living in your passion
  that we become a community of peace.
Grant us hope as we seek your mind,
  for it is in embodying your lowliness and humility
  that we come to care for others and serve in joy.

Grant us strength today as we seek your Spirit,
for it is in yielding to you that
we find rest and power in Christ.
It is in letting go that
we are free to be your children.

Bless us that we may be blessings to others.
Love us that we may love,
in the name of Jesus, Amen!

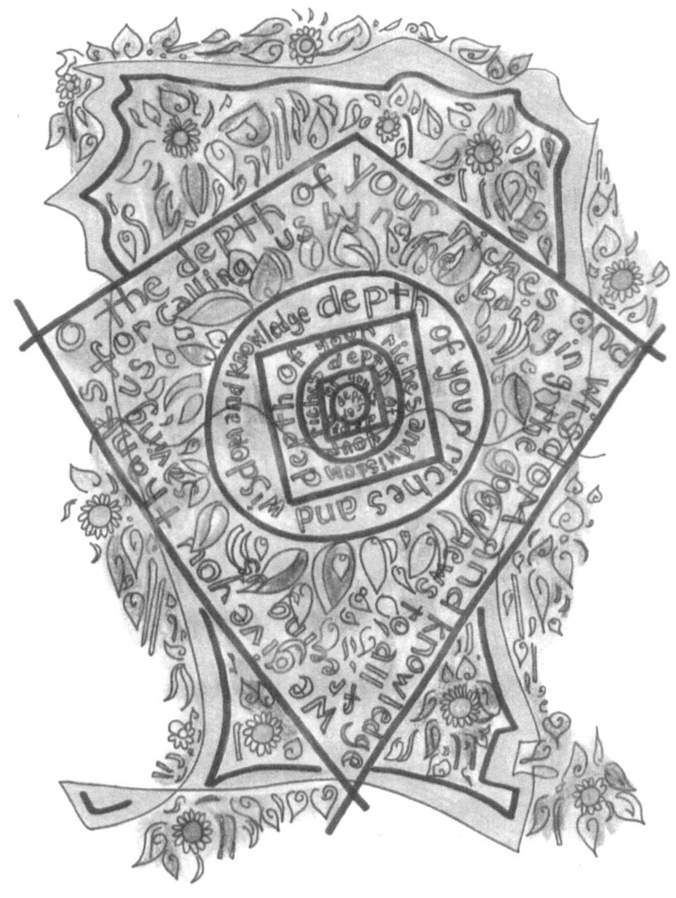

Obedience transports us to the depths of your *mysterium*

13

Obedience of Faith
(Romans)

Gracious God,
    O the depth of your riches and wisdom and knowledge!
How unsearchable are your judgments
    and how inscrutable your ways!
You have consigned all people to disobedience,
    that you may have mercy upon all!

We give you thanks
    for being just in judgment,
    slow in anger,
    and quick to welcome us.
Help us in the spirit of Christ welcome one another,
    love genuinely,
    hold fast to what is good,
    never flag in zeal,
    rejoice in hope,
    be patient in tribulation,
    be constant in prayer,
    contribute to the needs of the saints,
    practice hospitality.

We give you thanks for calling us by name,
    dying for us to offer the way of grace and salvation,
    saving us to be freed from death, sin, and cultural idols,
    and freeing us to be servants to righteousness and life!
We give you thanks for reconciling us through Christ,
    and adopting us to be your children.
You qualify us to be your ambassadors,
    bringing the good news to red, brown, black, white,
        and others,
    so that all might be brought to the obedience of faith.
To the only wise God
    be glory for evermore through Jesus Christ our Lord,
        Amen!

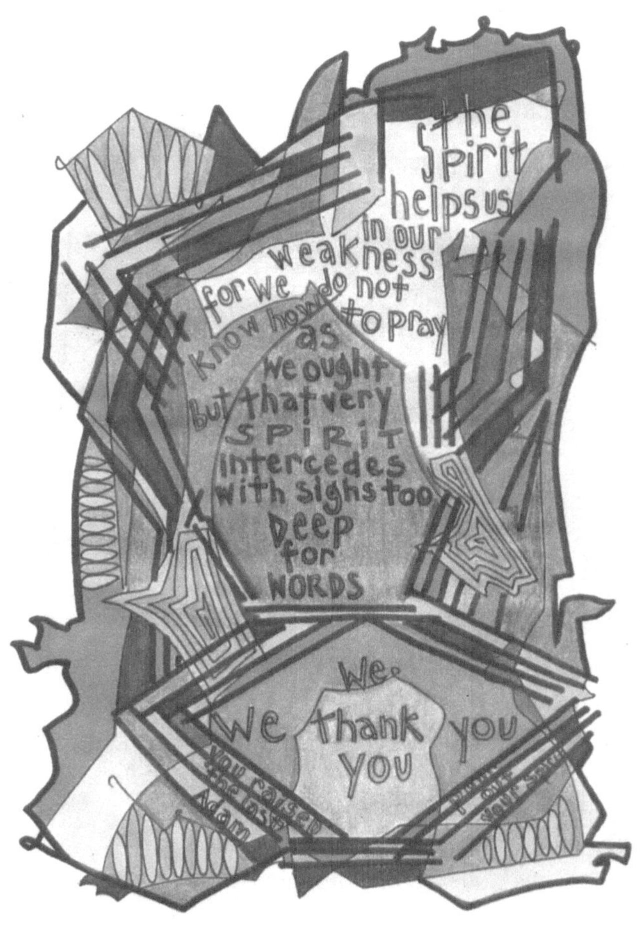

Revival of the Spirit
Divine Empathy,
the transformation of creation through Christ

14

Freedom in Christ
(Romans 5–8)

Gracious God,
we thank you that while we were yet sinners, Christ died for us,
the righteous for the unrighteous,
the holy for the cursed,
the honorable for the shameful,
so that in Christ you might set us right with you.

We thank you that while we were sinners in Adam,
Christ justified us:
the Second Adam tempted, yet sinless,
welcoming us to righteousness, faith, and salvation.
We thank you that while we were dead in Adam,
Christ quickened us to freedom.
You raised the Last Adam
whose resurrection triumphs over bondage,
whose resurrection power grants us life eternal,
and through your Son you adopt us.

Save us from our fallenness,
    thinking we can find freedom in boasting of ourselves,
        even as believers.
Shine on us to find the only path through Christ
    that we may find freedom
        from the bondage of religious rites
            and spiritual rules.
In Christ you have poured out your Spirit upon us,
    and blessed us as your beloved.
        In Christ's name, we pray. Amen!

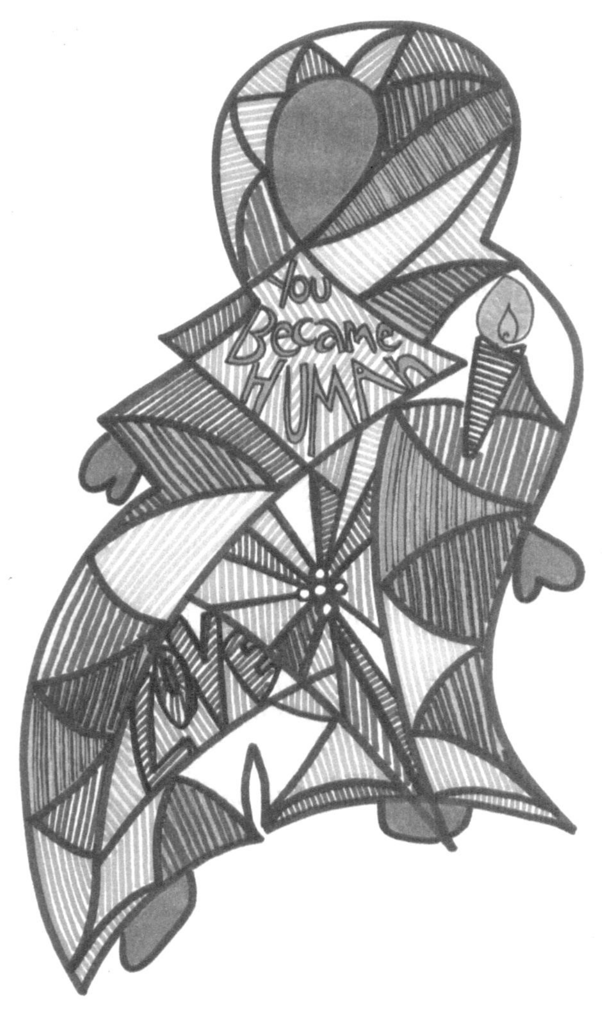

A divine coat of many colors
You took on flesh so that all may be clothed in your love

15

Crucified God, Lead Us to the Cross! (1 Corinthians)

"Let all that you do be done in love." (1 Cor 16:14)
"Let anyone be accursed who has no love for the Lord."
(1 Cor 16:22)

Crucified God,
have mercy on us when our culture becomes our idol.
Forgive us when we worship what our hands and minds
have made.
Lead us to the Cross to behold your glory,
the glory that critiques our conformity,
and challenges our complacency.

Have mercy on us when we boast of human reasoning.
Forgive us for glorifying ourselves,
thinking we can create divinity in our own image.
Lead us to the Cross of your wisdom,
the wisdom that is foolishness to the smart ones (Greek)
and stumbling blocks to the religious (Jews).

Have mercy on us when our egos are logs in our eyes.
  Forgive us for running over others
  and dividing the Body of Christ.
Lead us to the Cross
  to be stripped away by your love,
  and clothed by your humanity.

You became human because of love, patient and kind.
  A love that does not insist on its own way;
    not irritable or resentful,
    that rejoices in the right,
    that bears all things,
    believes all things,
    hopes all things,
    and endures all things.

Illumine our tunnel vision,
  short-sightedness,
  and broken dreams!
Lead us to the Cross to live in resurrection,
  the resurrection power that triumphs over sin,
  the resurrection hope that defeated the sting of death,
    through Christ, our Lord, we pray. Amen!

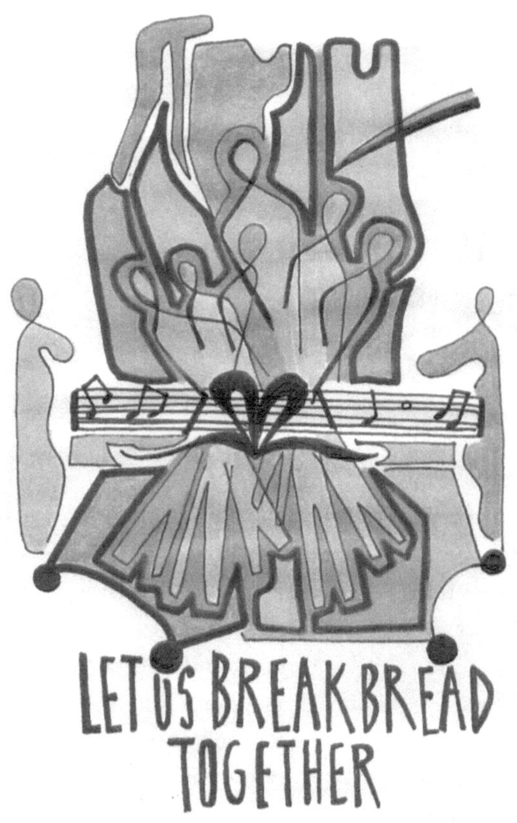

With music and meal
may we have a love feast

16

Love
(1 Cor 1:1–9; 13)

Gracious God, grant us wisdom
    that we might know your persistent grace.
Have mercy on us
    that we might be kind to others.
Be patient with us
    that we might empathize with one another.
Show us the more excellent way of love
    that we might build up the community.
As we break bread this morning,
    may your Word make sacred that which is common in
        our lives.
Inspire us to see this local community of faith as your body,
    so that in worship we may love you,
    in service we may love our neighbor,
    in prayer we may know your will,
    and humbly calling on your name,
        we may esteem others better than ourselves,
    through Christ our Lord, Amen!

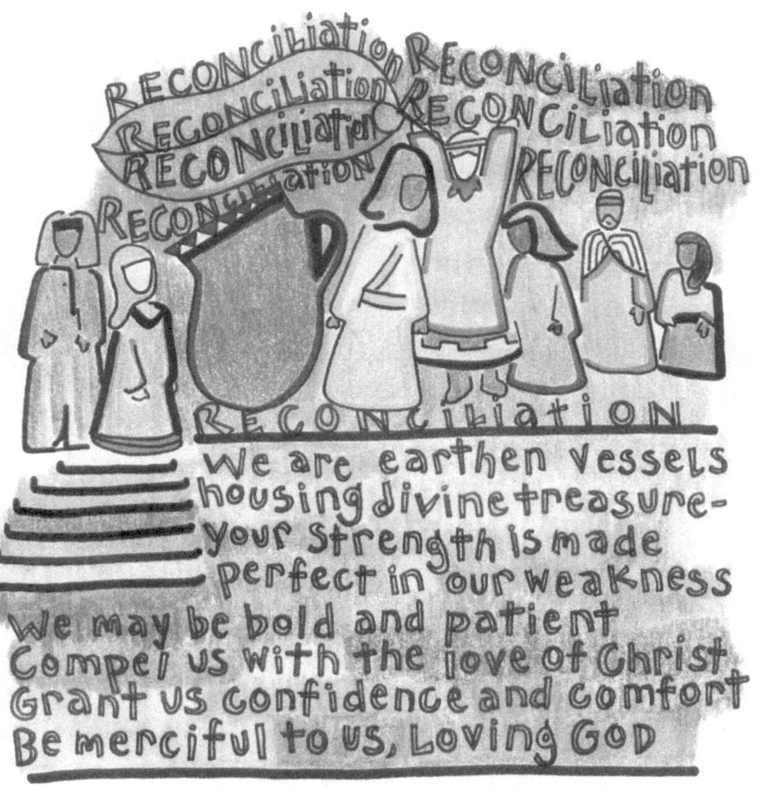

We, the rainbow, are your earthen vessels

17

Ministry of Reconciliation (2 Corinthians)

Forgive us, Merciful God,
    for boasting in our strength
    believing we are superhuman.
Forbid us
    for dwelling on the letter of the law
    and using force when your kingdom calls for love.
Make us transparent servants of Christ,
    so that all may receive your gospel of the new covenant
        as true,
    for we are letters of recommendation written by your
        Spirit.

Forgive us, Merciful God,
    for losing our minds.
    We forget who we are,
        we crown ourselves and rob you of glory.
Almighty God,
    you have made us neither dirt nor divine,
        but earthen vessels, housing divine treasure.

Remind us,
that we are ambassadors for Christ despite the thorns of our flesh,
Remind us,
that your strength is made perfect in our weakness.

Teach us, today,
how to be Christ's aroma to those who are being saved and among those who are perishing,
so that your gospel might reconcile our brokenness.
Teach us to learn from our Master Jesus,
who was crucified in weakness,
but lives by the power of God.
Teach us to learn from our Lord Jesus,
who was rich, yet for our sake he became poor
so that we who are destitute might be blessed with bountiful grace.

Be merciful to us, Loving God,
do not break our spirits when we are timid, in doubt, or in pain;
grant us confidence and comfort.
Compel us with the love of Christ,
may we live for you,
trusting in your competence,
bold in your service,
patient like all your apostles.
We pray all these things in Christ's name. Amen!

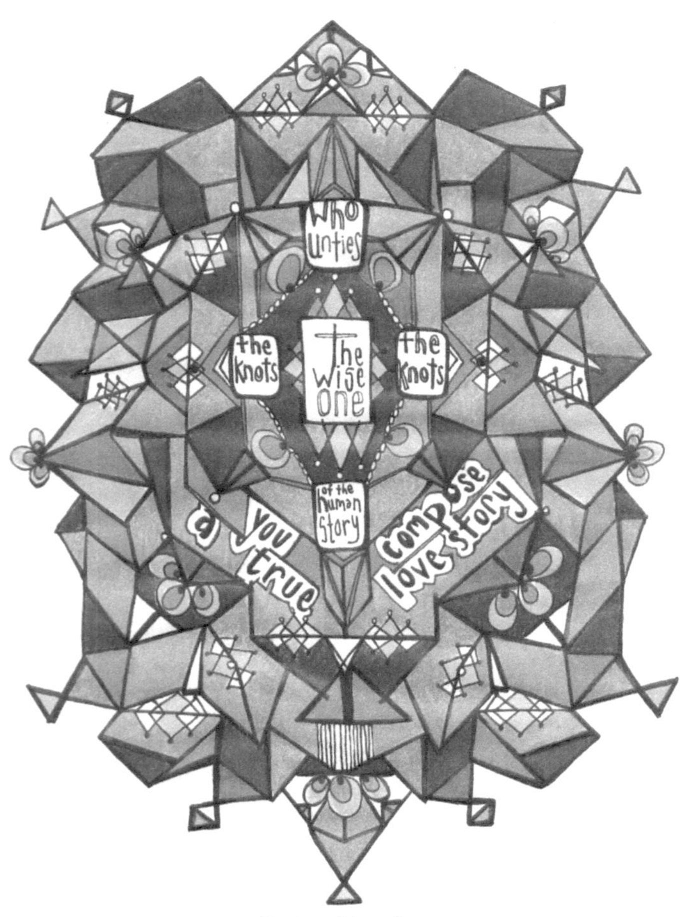

Stained in glass
claimed by the Christly composition of history

18

One in You
(Galatians)

Blessed are you, the Holy One,
    for you do not coerce,
    you welcome us with your suffering love.
You rule the cosmos,
    you reign and sustain our trust,
    for you subvert the power of the strong,
        and empower the weak.

Teach us today to live out the vision-hope of your Paradise
        of that Day,
    when lions and lambs lay side by side,
    enemies and foes shake hands,
    kings and masters are slaves to you,
    and the destitute sit at the bosom of Abraham.

Blessed are you, the Incarnate of God,
    for you walked our path from the manger to the Cross,
    leading us to the kingdom law, the Law of Love.
You reconciled the elements of the world,
    embodying the curse of sin.

You untied the knots of the human story,
as the Anointed One of God, the end (purpose)
of history.
You composed a true love story,
birthing the church and embracing your beloved.

Blessed are you, the Wise One.
Blessed be your liberating grace.
Your mercy encapsulates us,
your love transfuses us,
and your Spirit restores us with gentleness,
through your Holy name, Jesus Christ, Amen!

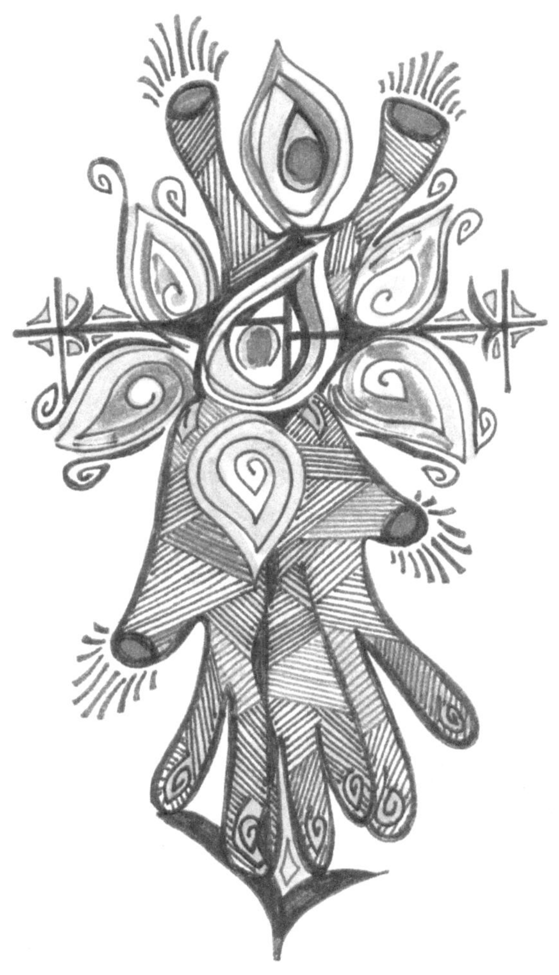

Spirit-filled hands and feet of Christ

19

Your Humanity, Our Divinity (Galatians)

Gracious God,
have mercy on us
when our hearts turn cold,
when war and injustice are so common that they trouble us no more,
when we think Israelis cannot co-exist with Palestinians in the city of peace.

Have mercy on us
when we think we are religious by loving you without loving our neighbors,
when we treat neighbors as burdens and respect colleagues only dutifully,
when we turn cynical because of the haunting past and overwhelming now.

Have mercy on us
when we have sight but no vision,
when fear paralyzes and hope is utopia,
when the Cross does not shake us,
the crucifixion no more a stigma,

the resurrection a myth.
Gracious God,
may your faith be our righteousness,
your hope our vision,
your love our doxology,
your image our humanness (as community)
and your humanity, our divinity,
through Christ our Lord, Amen!

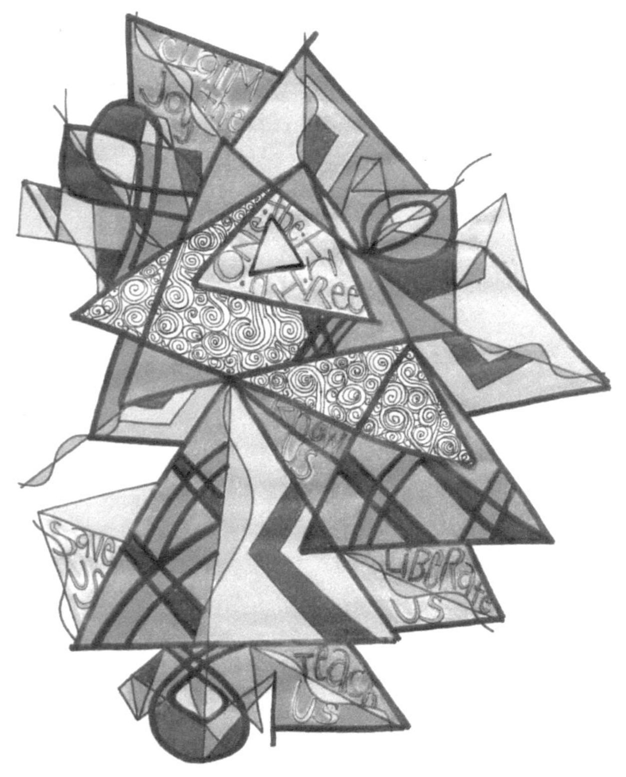

Liberate, save, teach, and know us, Trinity!

20

Source of Our Being
(Ephesians)

Source of our being,
  we worship you,
    for you come to us in Jesus, in your Word,
      and in your Spirit.
Source of salvation, wisdom, and hope,
  we come to you
    for you are the God of grace who gives generously,
      every good and perfect gift.

Spirit of Truth,
  save us from the scholarship that is dogmatic
    or agnostic,
  baptize us in the font of your mystery, knowledge,
    and humility.
Liberate us from despair in performing research
      and writing footnotes,
  teach us to be careful and articulate,
  and trust the fruits of a good scholarship as divine gifts
    for the church and the world.

Help us to know your design for creation and your ordering
for our lives,
as you have revealed to us in your self-giving love,
through Christ our Lord.

Blessed are you,
the Three in One of Unity and One in Three
of Communion,
for showing us that life is not independence,
but community,
that to be human is to be in relationships
engendering peace and security and trust.
Forbid us to be computer clones, cold logic, or super-mind.
But to live out the Trinitarian life of communion,
to be warm blooded creatures,
to claim the joy and pain of one another,
in the name of the self-emptying One
yet overflowing Love, Amen!

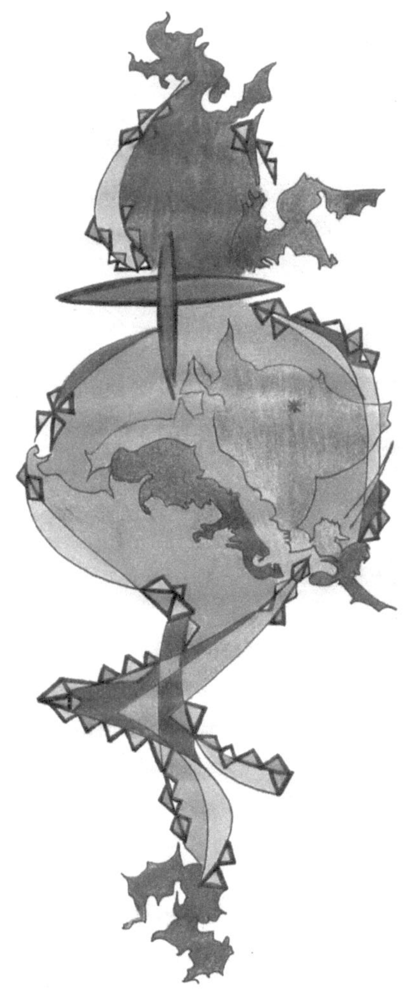

The world is enraptured by the Word

21

Cosmic Christ
(Ephesians, Colossians)

Gracious God,
you chose us in Christ before the creation of the world.
We give thanks that it is not by our will or works,
but through the faithfulness of Christ that you shape our destiny.
You predestine us in love and adopt us as your children,
not according to our status or beauty,
but according to the Son's glory.

We thank you for your forgiveness,
for saving us from sin and the curse of death,
through the riches of your bountiful grace.
We thank you for lavishing upon us,
students of your Word, wisdom and understanding.
You enlighten our studies according to your good pleasure.

Choose us still, God, that we might imitate the boldness of Christ,
predestine us, that we might taste the goodness of Christ.

Forgive us, that we might love you,
empower us to worship you through our diligent
scholarship.
For the faithfulness of Christ is more trustworthy than
our own faith,
the taste of your goodness is sweeter than life itself,
the power of mercy defeats the tyranny
of condemnation,
and the end of theology is the beginning of doxology.

Gracious God,
in a world of broken vision,
allow us to behold the image of Christ,
the invisible God, the firstborn of all creation.
In a quick fix world of constant conflicts,
bid us to recall how you have created for Christ
in whom all things hold together,
and meld us as one mosaic in you.
Above all, in a world of dashed hope and false security,
help us witness the cosmic Christ at work through
the Cross—Christ, the great assurance.
Praise be to you, God and Father of our Lord Jesus Christ,
who has blessed us with every spiritual blessing
in Christ, Amen!

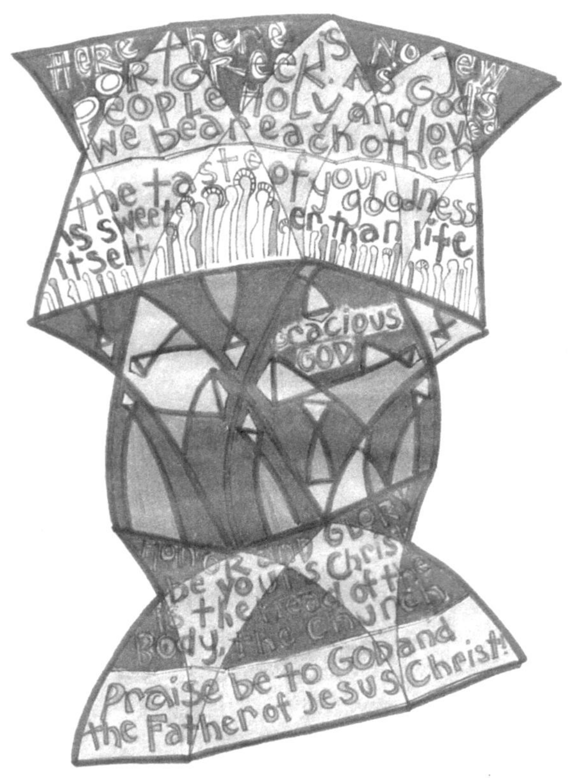

Meld us as one mosaic, Lord!

22

Global Church
(Ephesians)

By your grace, we (have) learn(ed)
to bend our knees at your Cross,
to stretch our minds with your mystery,
to fill our hearts with your love,
to offer our voices to your glory,
to extend our hands to bless our neighbors,
and to walk in your path.
Instruct us that
the end of theology is the beginning of our doxology
(being known by you),
the end of doxology is our faith (knowing you fully),
the end of faith is living in your mysterious love
and wondrous grace.

Blessed be the God and Father of our Lord Jesus Christ,
who blessed us in Christ with every spiritual blessing,
who chose us in Christ before the foundation
of the world,
who destined us in love to be your children
through Jesus Christ,
who redeemed us through Christ's blood,

who lavished upon us riches of your grace,
who made known to us in all wisdom the mystery
of your will,
who set forth a plan to unite all things in Christ,
who destined us to live for the praise of your glory,
and who sealed us with the promise of Holy Spirit
those who heard the Word of truth and believed
in Christ.

Praise you for incarnating as human
out of your divinity.
Magnify you for incarnating the church
as the body of Christ through your transcendence.
We worship you for emptying yourself on the Cross,
though you are all in all.

Show us the way of peace and reconciliation,
teach us the way of redeeming love.
Reveal the plan of salvation so long hidden,
embolden us through our faith in Christ.
Sustain the unity of the Spirit among us--
between Jews and Gentiles,
husbands and wives,
children and parents,
masters and slaves.
Oh, that we might comprehend the height and depth
of Christ's love,
that we may be made whole!
Prompt us to confess and proclaim the your art
of the Trinitarian community:
one hope according to our call,

one Lord, one faith, one baptism, one God
    and Father of us all,
who is above all and through all and in all. Alleluia!

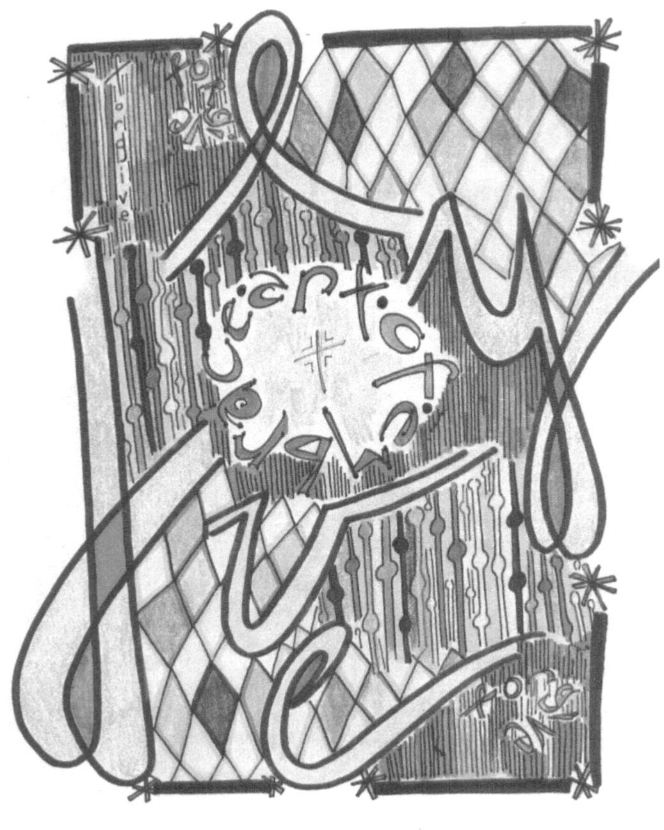

The art of embrace
with love and joy, rejoice in the Lord always!

23

Love and Joy
(Philippians and Philemon)

Gracious Lord,
    teach us to have ears that hear your voice,
    hands that wish to give rather than receive,
    hearts that beat for the least and the lost.
Speak to us, Lord, that we might live;
    teach us the art of embrace,
    the pain of forgiveness,
    and the joy of being forgiven.
Gather us at the Cross
    that we might find the intersection of our humanity and divinity.

Gracious Lord,
    forgive us for having friends we treat as aliens,
    forgive us for having feet slow to seek the gospel,
    forgive us for being your workers blind to joy.
Train us to live your gospel,
    welcoming our enemies to your table,
    with confidence that your wounded love has made us whole.
Break open to us the whole biblical story of salvation:

the theological language of creation,
and the liberating Cross
    even where your beloved Son reveals your love
        to us, Amen!

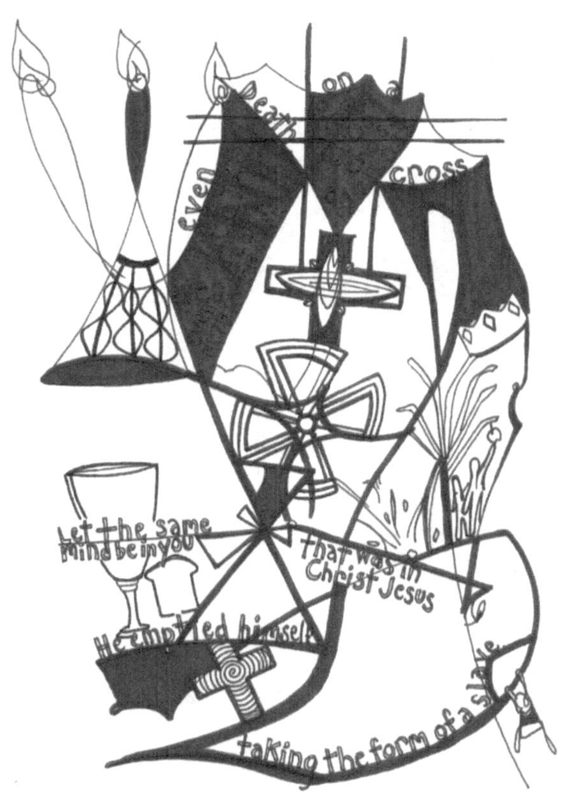

. . . even death on a Cross . . .

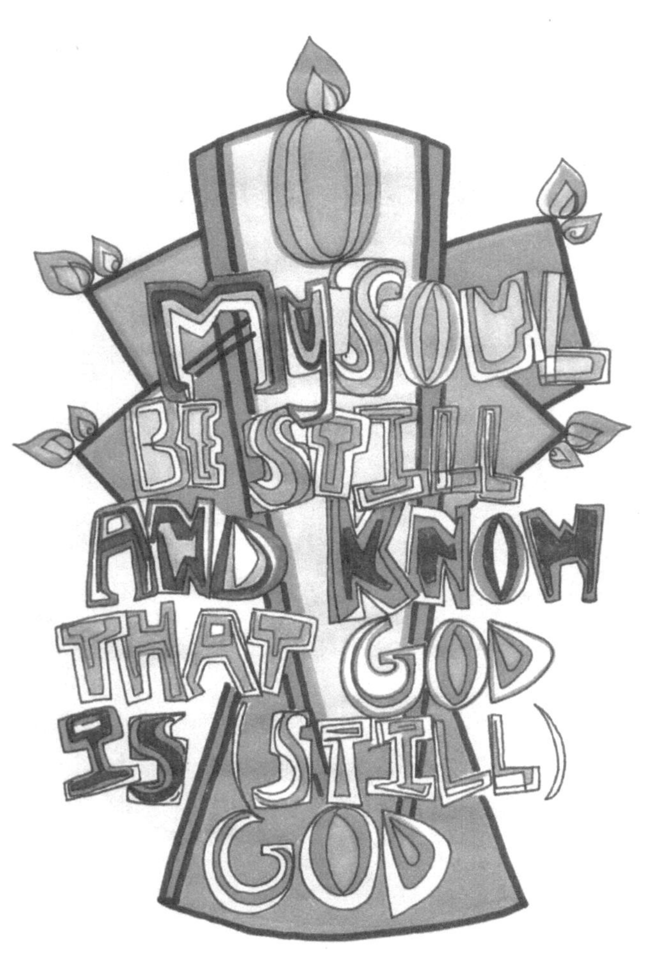

Changeless
God is *still* God

24

Hope in the Coming God (1 and 2 Thessalonians)

O my soul,
be still and know that God is still, and still God he is.

We worship you, Eternal God for who you are,
the great I AM, the changing changeless One,
the transcendent and immanent One,
the nameless Word that speaks forth life,
the invisible One taking human form,
the Creator embodying the image of a slave,
the Holy One sharing all the conditions of humanity,
yet without sin,
the God before and beyond history, and yet in history,
the Body and Blood that creates, redeems,
and sustains all.
We worship you, Loving God for who you are,
the God of life who displays goodness and beauty
in your creation for our sake,
who demonstrated bountiful grace in the fullness
of Christ's humanity,
who shows forth extravagant love for us on the Cross,
who proves that death cannot define our destiny.

Truly God and truly Human, we worship you,
you have shown that divine and human can be one,
you teach us to be fully human is to be faithful.
We worship you, Coming God, for who you are,
for you are the God of Alpha and Omega,
and your presence empowers history with meaning,
your presence rests with us when we are in pain.

Strengthen us, today, God of creation,
to trust that abundant life is the divine gift
and imperative, and not a choice.
Free us, today, God of redemption,
for your will for us is salvation rather than judgment,
sanctification rather than despair.
Grace us, today, God of consummation,
for the goal of history is salvation,
as the end of history is defined by your Messiah,
who brings whole of history unto you.
Allow us not to bow to idols of power, domination, sin
and suffering.

Grant us the wisdom that was revealed in the passion
of your Son Jesus Christ,
so that we may live to love always
knowing wound of love triumphs over evil of violence.
Grant us faith in times of trial and testing,
so that we may live to trust you.
Grant us assurance and rest in times of tribulation
and persecution,
so that we may live to hope always
knowing we are destined to salvation and wholeness.

Thank you for being the faithful God who
destines us to wholeness, elects us as your beloved,
calls us to be your ambassadors.
All glory, honor, power be yours, forever and ever, Amen!

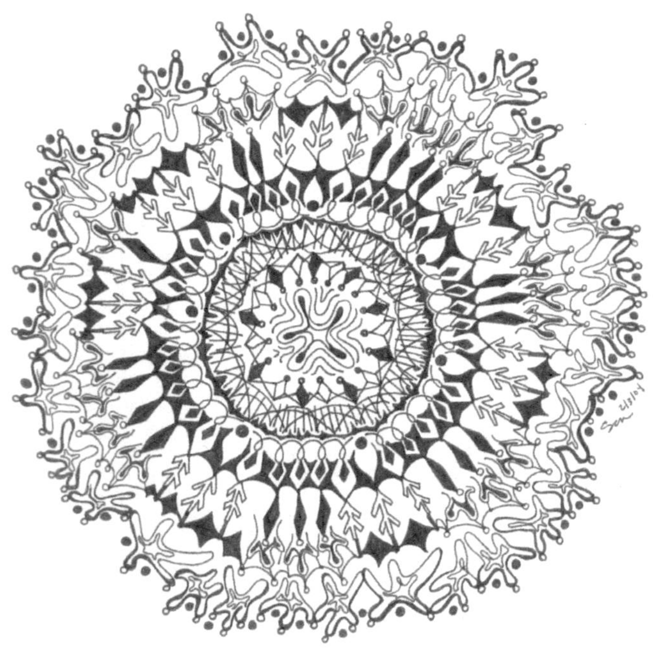

. . . that we may be humble before you

25

Sincere Faith and Good Conscience (Pastoral Epistles)

Holy God,
    grant us wisdom to know the truth,
    and the courage to proclaim it
        in the midst of die-hard, dogmatic conviction
            of our modern society,
        in the flux of relative, unsure postmodern ethos,
        and in the secular agnostic mindset.
Yet, even in our boldness, grant us mercy,
    that we may be teachable, humble, and fearful
        before you,
    for we stand always in your presence
    at your judgment, correction, and testing.
    in need of your grace.

Righteous God,
    give us not only the knowledge of your truth,
    but also the simplicity to know your goodness
    and to walk the Christian talk.
Grant us joy to live a right and purposeful life
    in the midst of moral confusions.

Yet, be merciful to us, we pray,
    that we may be compassionate,
    ready to listen,
    and quick to empathize,
    for you are our gracious Savior
        manifested in the flesh,
        vindicated in the Spirit,
        taken up in glory.

God of creation,
    keep our sincere faith,
    to follow you in good conscience,
    and to love our neighbors with a pure heart,
        for the sake of Christ, Amen!

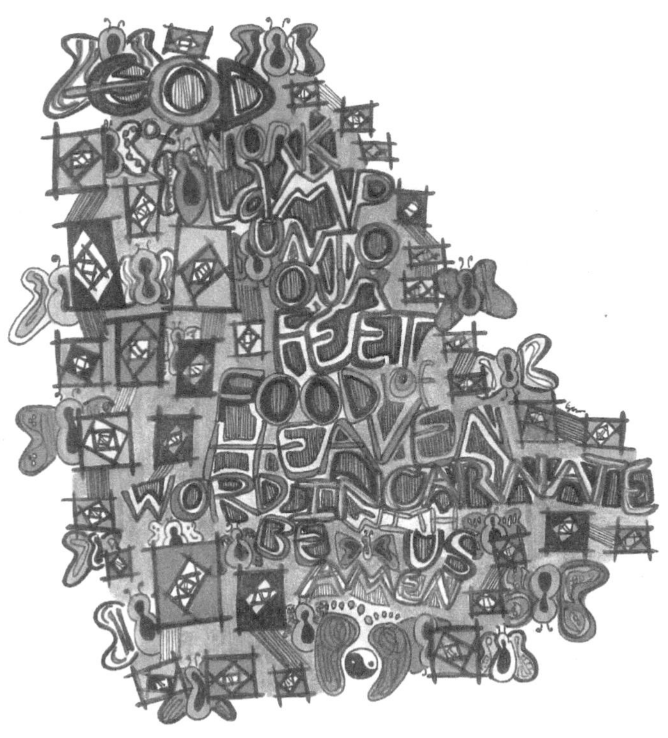

Guide us, feed us, be with us

26

God of Yin and Yang
(Hebrews)

The eternal Logos that became flesh,
    we worship you!
The humanity of your Son has embodied your divinity,
    and your humanity is our divinity.
Thank you for bringing all things into existence
        through logos,
    that we may name you.
No word will ever be able to capture your Living Word,
    yet, with human language you privilege us
        to express your Truth, Alleluia!

God of Word and Silence, teach us to name you,
    for in naming you we name ourselves;
    may we also to worship you in your mystery.
Your Speech has pierced our thoughts and healed
        our wounds;
    your Silence has freed us to worship you
        as your Spirit leads.
Self-revealing and Elusive God,
    your presence awaits us,
    your absence makes us wait,

your presence lifts us up with joy and love,
your absence draws us forth with awe and fear.
Embrace us with your mystery,
that we may live as your children, loving and trusting.
God of transcendence and immanence,
guide the language of our reason,
and teach us the grammar of faith,
that we may live in the wisdom
of the sacred tradition
and speak your prophetic utterance.

God of work and rest,
empower us to plant and care for the living Word
of your vineyard,
lead us to till the soil of justice and love
as you rain down your mercy and blessing upon all.
Grant us sabbath rest as we live in communion with you
and become your light in the world.

Lamp unto our feet,
guide us,
Food of heaven,
feed us,
Word Incarnate,
be with us,
in Jesus' name, Amen!

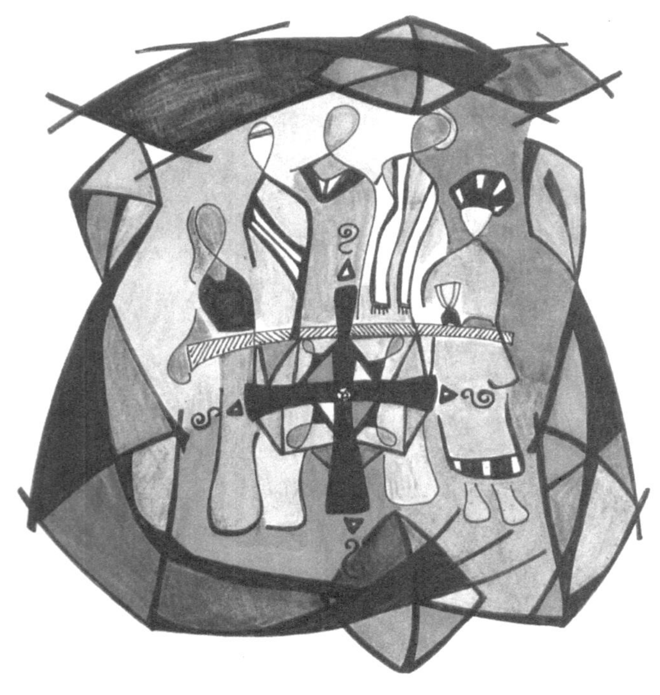

Friendship of Sophia in communion

27

You are Our Wisdom of Perfection (James)

When we were in our mothers' wombs,
we heard of your whispering and felt your impulse,
not knowing you are the Ancient of Days,
the Father of Lights.
The water and the Spirit bathed us to life, birthed us to joy—
the first nine months and the many innocent years,
how blissful it was then not knowing
your prevenient grace!

In our rebellious teens and "grown-up" years,
we do not know why life becomes a puzzle and a pain.
We look for answers—to the problems of sin, injustice,
suffering,
but we seldom hear your voice.
We seek you,
not knowing you are always in front of us.

At those dark nights we wrestle with you, the Holy One,
you make us whole every time we encounter you.

Wisdom, you speak in and as silence.
you are as far as the Aries (Lamb) and as near
as our breath.
You draw near to us before we have the courage to draw
near to you.

In faith of our Lord Jesus Christ, we pray for what
we have not seen,
groan for what we cannot name,
and hope for what is not here yet—
it is our praying for the impossible for ourselves
and the world only you the Sophia can realize.
Assured by your Spirit who befriends us and prays
on our behalf
in the divine soliloquy of the Triune Community—
and there
we are embraced as your own and become
your Body on earth.

Keep us connected to you, O Lord,
and unite us to others and to ourselves.
As we ask for forgiveness as much as we forgive,
knowing how you have healed us
in our honoring of others.

Translate the aesthetic relationship we have with you
into poetic justice,
as we channel your love and order into mercy
and justice to the world.
Move us to be compassionate and responsible beings,
as we imitate Christ to offer ourselves to be your gift

for others—
and we in turn are blessed.
God of goodness,
we thank you for blessing us with pure and perfect gifts.
Life is like a mist,
and will be in vain if it is without your will and purpose.
Train us to dance with the movement of your hands,
which protect and bless the sequence and rhythm of life.

Grant us the big picture and long view of life,
and have mercy on us when we reduce ourselves
to less than human,
when we trash your image.
Forbid us to slice life into fractures of envy and fear
and greed.
Your Law has invigorated our freedom
that we may love you and our neighbor naturally,
for your mercy trumps judgment and arrogance,
your righteousness triumphs over rage,
your shalom resolves conflict.

Grant us patience and virtue to live in the tension
and ambiguity of life,
trusting that life may be rotten, but God,
you are always good.
Touch us with your wisdom, Sophia,
for you have inhabited the cosmos with beauty
and order,
rendering us forever yours.

God of Word Eternal,
    blessed be your name,
    for you have taught us to court you,
        to spend time with you,
        to listen to you,
        and to see your creative Word at work—
            the Word invisible that was made flesh,
            eternally personified as Wisdom,
            demonstrated as goodness,
            and embodied as superabundant life.
Praying in the Wisdom who dwells in all, Amen!

Shalom. Wholeness. Perfection.

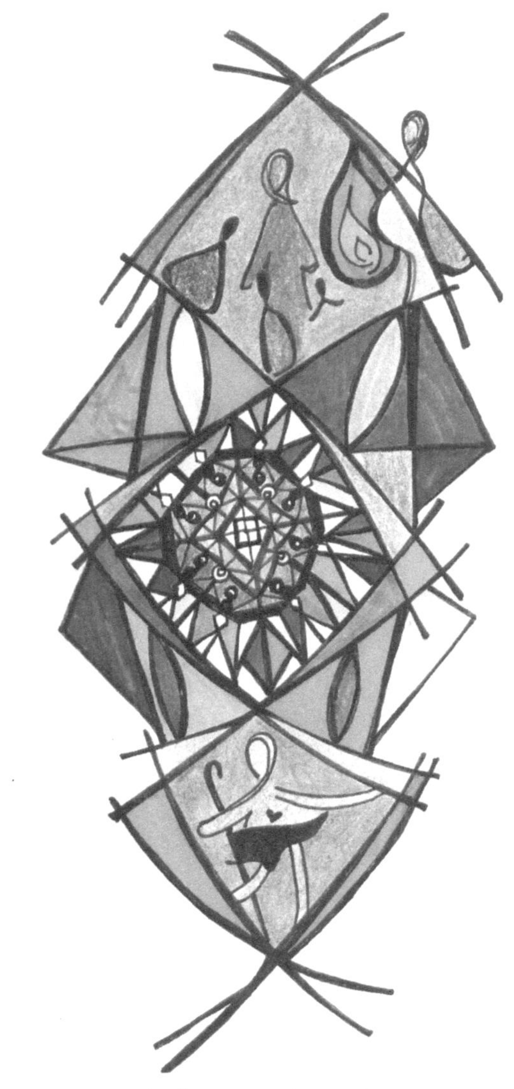

Birthed anew in living hope

28

Discernment and Faithfulness (Jude, 1–2 Peter)

Blessed be the God and Father of our Lord Jesus Christ,
    whose precious blood was destined spotless
        before the foundation of the world!
For you have birthed us anew
    in living hope through Christ's resurrection.
You have given us an imperishable inheritance,
    and guarded us for your salvation.
Grant us genuine faith that is more precious than gold,
    standing the test of any fire.
Sober our minds,
    set our eyes on Christ,
    attune our hearts to his suffering
    that even in our trials we might rejoice.

Merciful God,
    help us to contend for the faith, once
        and for all delivered to the saints,
    as we claim Jesus Christ as Lord.
Build us up on the most holy faith,
    to pray in the Holy Spirit,
    to keep ourselves in the love of God,
    and to wait for the mercy of our Lord Jesus Christ
        unto eternal life.

Gracious God, keep us from falling.
With Christ through the Spirit,
be all glory, majesty, dominion, and authority,
before all time and now and for ever, Amen!

The word-path of the Cross
Dear God, may we abide in you together

29

Fellowship of Love
(1–3 John)

Dear God,
when we think we are righteous,
do not be angry with us,
show us your throne;
when we think we are just,
be patient with us,
show us your sacrifice on the Cross;
when we are deceitful,
be merciful to us,
show us your faithfulness and truthfulness;
when we retreat to darkness,
reveal your glory;
when we consider death our destiny,
breathe into us,
show us life.
When we divide community in violence,
forgive us,
show us your tears at Jerusalem and Gethsemane;
when we wish to be less than human and whole,
do not give up on us, O Lord,
illumine your image among us.

God of righteousness,
    convict us of our sins that we might turn to you.
God of justice,
    judge our wrongs that we might be humble.
God of truth,
    speak your mind to us that we might trust in your truth.
God of light,
    shine your light upon our feet that we might walk
        in your path.
God of life,
    draw us to have fellowship with you that we might
        have eternal life.
God of love,
    with your passion guide us to compassion.
God of perfection,
    abide in us that we might abide in you,
        through Christ our Lord, Amen!

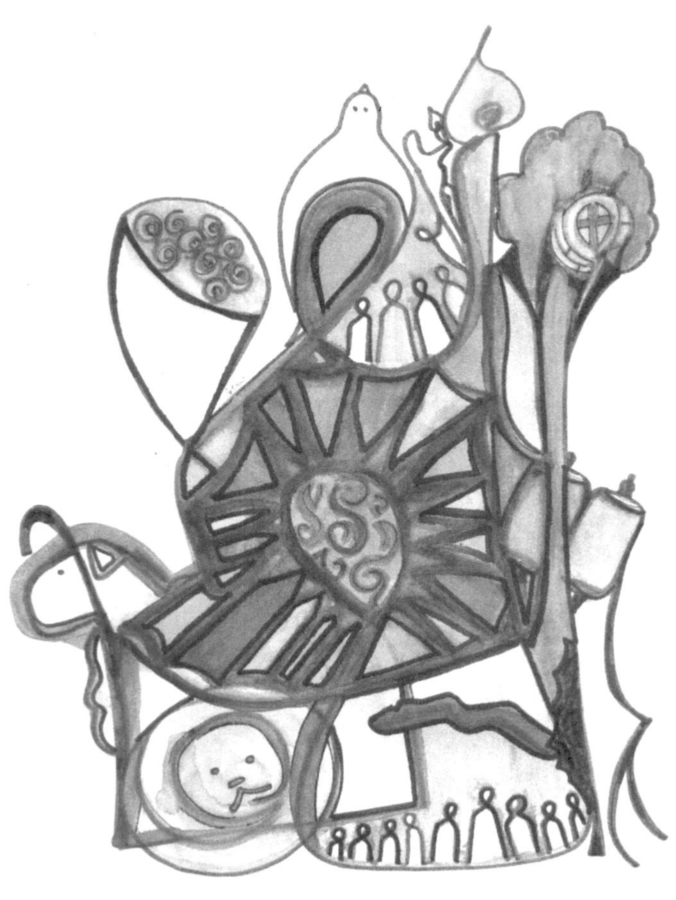

Restoration on the wings of the dove
The lion learns to lie with the lamb

30

Dove and Lamb of God, Lift Us Up (Philemon and Revelation)

Be merciful to us, Lord,
    when we are confused, boastful, and lost,
    when we are aggressive as lions, proud as eagles.
In our fear, we cringe and hold our palms tight,
    but are often holding onto thin air.
In distrust, we boast and we pump our muscles to strike,
    but we are dying of anemia.
In insecurity, we build the Great Wall
        and Homeland Security,
    but in the end we are only paralyzed by prejudice
            and pride.

Dove of God, lift us up from the dust
    that we may soar in your Spirit to face your light.
From the depth of primordial sea to the fallenness
        at the Garden (of Eden),
    your wings have redeemed and created.
From the Jordan River of this earth to the River of Life
        in the new heaven,
    you have breathed new life and baptized
        your children as your beloved.

From Mount Sinai to the Hill of Golgotha,
    your Dove has deconstructed all boastings (lions)
        and dethroned all Empires (eagles).

Lamb of God,
    forbid us to boast of our military,
    our economy, and our knowledge.
Help us not to confuse meekness with weakness,
    silence with consensus,
    domination with power.
Almighty God,
    you have stooped down to meet us at Nazareth--
        the lowest point of the planet earth,
    for your lowliness defines your honor (glory).
Gracious Friend,
    you have lived among the human plots
        with self-sacrificial love;
    your servitude defines your humanity.
Impartial Judge,
    you have given us the Torah as the way of life,
    and embodied the Torah in your opening palm,
        blessing all with your grace,
        for your faithfulness and mercy define your power.
We worship you, Dove and Lamb of God, Amen!

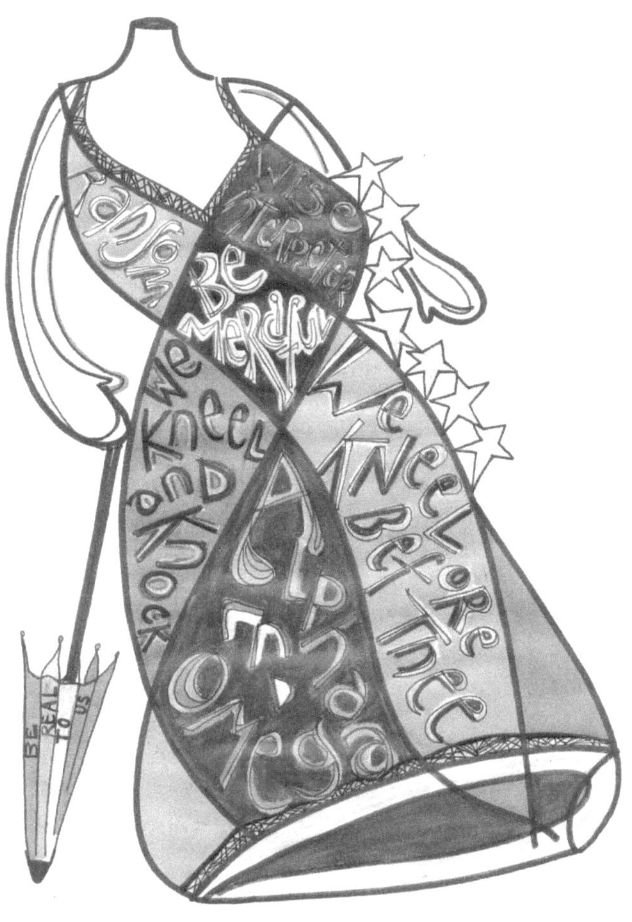

Godly glamour
Transform our excess into your forever "yes"

31

Alleluia
(Revelation)[2]

1. Living God, the God "who is and who was
        and who is to come,"
    you are the divine author of world history,
        the wise interpreter,
        the redemptive actor,
        the producer of our meaningful life-stories.
Grant us victory without a second death,
    include our names in the book of life.
Have mercy on us as we learn to be faithful,
    as we kneel and listen before you, Holy Spirit.

2. Loving God, the God "who dies and was raised f
        or evermore,"
    you hold the keys of Death and Hades.
Be merciful to us as we suffer for your name's sake.
    Keep us from weariness as we keep our first love for you.
We kneel before you and listen to you, Holy Spirit,
    and pray that you would grant us the tree of life
        in your paradise.

---

2. This prayer is written in seven verses, in accordance to the many linguistic and symbolic sevens of the book of Revelation, among which are the seven names of God, Christ, Spirit, etc.

3. God who “sits on the throne,”
    you are the God who rules with your Word,
        the sharp two-edged sword.
Be truth for us,
    that we might be true to others!
May we be accountable in community,
    for you judge evils and dominations,
    and you redeem those in suffering pain.
Teach us to be faithful to your Word and repent of our sins,
    for you reign with sacrificial love.
We kneel before you and listen to you, Holy Spirit,
    and pray that you would grant us the morning star.

4. The Coming One,
    you are forever, far as the star yet close as our breath,
    you are forever illusive, yet constantly knocking.
Be real to us!
    For you are the God who cares,
    the God who is in control of the goal, the purpose,
        and the process of history.
Teach us to be watchful,
    holding fast to your Word
    and putting on a clean garment (living in your will
        of sanctification)
    until you come, Lord Jesus.
We kneel before you and listen to you, Holy Spirit,
    and pray that you would grant us hidden manna,
        white stone, white garment, and new name.

5. "The Alpha and the Omega,"
the one who has the key of David,
who opens doors no one shall shut, who shuts doors
no one can open.
You are the beginning and the end of all things.
Satan, with his lies, temptations, resistance
and destruction, is but
a second in eternity,
a dust compared with your divinity,
a fool compared with your wisdom,
a vanity compared with your power.
Let us bow down before you, Triune God,
for you will bring the whole creation to yourself
through Christ.
We kneel before you and listen to you, Holy Spirit,
and pray to become pillars for your temple
in the heavenly City of God.
We pray to be permanent residents of the new Jerusalem,
built upon the foundation of Christ.

6. "The Lord God Almighty,"
God of Amen, the forever "yes,"
the God of the faithful and true witness.
Allow us to see that we are needy, wretched, naked;
keep our hearts near to yours, and warm our hearts
to your holiness.
Grant us gold refined by fire.
Love us, reprove us, anoint us, cleanse us.
We kneel before the door of your temple and knock,
for you have been knocking on our doors of fear
and seclusion, hatred and violence.
You graciously invite us to feast with you
at the eschatological banquet.

7. To Christ, "the Lamb of God," together
with seven spirits of God,
who holds seven stars and walks among
the seven golden lamp-stands,
worthy are you to take the scroll and to open its seals.
You were slain and by blood
you ransom people from God from every tribe
tongue and people and nation.
We thank you for loving us (the sinners and the faithful
witnesses),
for freeing us from our sins by your blood
and making us a people of your kingdom,
priests to your God and Father.
Worthy is the Lamb who was slain,
to receive power and wealth and wisdom and might
and honor and glory and blessing,
for ever and ever, Amen!

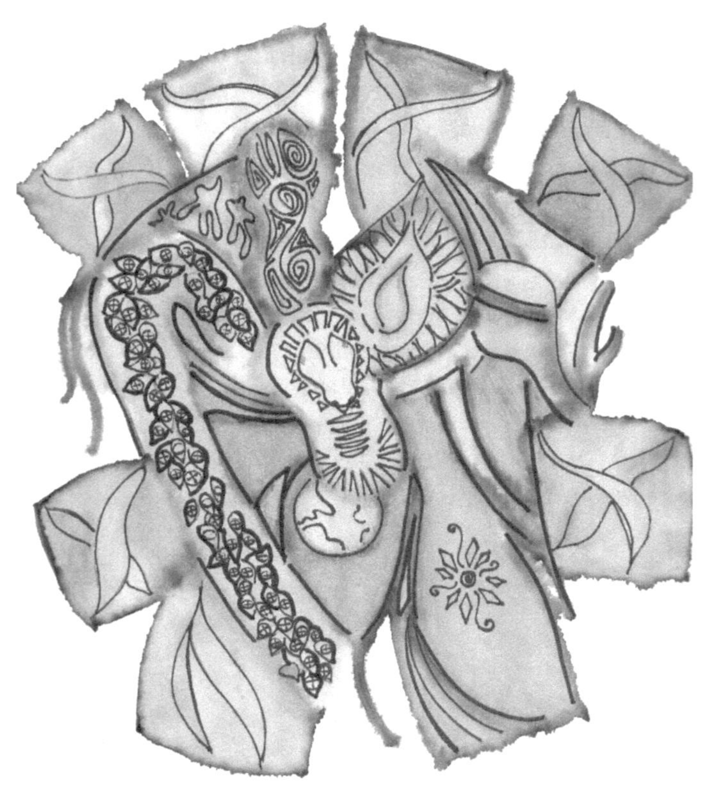

Pattern us by your light

32

Lead Us On . . . For Your Service (A Litany at Commencement; New Testament Theology)[3]

LEADER

All baptized Christians are called to share in Christ's
ministry of love and service in the world,
to the glory of God and for the redemption
of the human family and the whole of creation.

UNISON PRAYER

We thank you, Eternal God,
for creating each one of us, wonderfully made
for your purpose,
and loved at great cost by your Son, for the sake
of your church and the world.

---

3. This prayer is used at the end of the two courses: the New Testament Survey and New Testament Theology. It serves two purposes. First, it provides a theological summary of the New Testament books in the form of prayer, thus the present form retains the square brackets of New Testament books for pedagogy purposes. Thus, names of New Testament books are not to be read when this litany of prayer is said. Second, it serves as a sending forth of the group, as readers bless each other in the form of litany benediction and affirmation of their respective Christian ministry. The beginning and ending of this prayer is adapted from "Order for the Ordination of Elders," The United Methodist Book of Worship (Nashville: The United Methodist Publishing House, 1992), 23, 38.

LEADER

You who seek to lead and teach in Christ's church
are to love, serve, and pray for all the people
among whom you work,
caring like for young and old, strong and weak, rich
and poor.
Remember that you are called to serve rather than
to be served.

Will you be steadfast disciples of Christ,
so that your lives may be fashioned by the gospel,
and provide faithful examples for all God's people?

CLASS

We will, with the help of the Triune God,
and all that we have learned in scripture, in reading,
and in class.

PRAYER LITANY

(class says words in plain type, leader says words in script)

Lord,
Imprint upon our lives the life of Christ:
the Great Teacher and Doer of the higher righteousness,
whose mercy makes the yoke of the law light
and restful [Matthew].
the Crucified God whose pain and death on the Cross
transcend miracles and resurrection,
and whose passion models for us servant leadership
with trust [Mark].

the Universal Savior whose forgiveness reaches out
to Samaritans, women, outcasts
in whom your salvation and unbounded love
are witnessed by the whole world [Luke-Acts].
the Logos Christ whose eternal presence, incarnation
and constant dialogues with God challenge us
to be light of the world and spiritual signs
in our community [John].

Infect us with the radical gospels of Christ to transform
our lives:
that we may turn away from all forms of cultural boasting
and toward the building of "God's beloved"
in the obedience of faith [Romans].
that we may eliminate individualism
and build communities equalized through love
[1 Corinthians].
that we may tear off the masks of superheroes
and humbly practice the ministry of reconciliation
[2 Corinthians].

God in Christ,
grant us greater visions for the church, the Body of Christ
in the world today:
Instill in us the spirit of freedom
to live in Christ as your children and the children
of Abraham and Sarah
through the Spirit [Galatians].
Instill in us the spirit of joy
so that, drawn together by the Cross,

we may serve you as one Body and friendship
with one another [Philippians].
Invite us in the spirit of discernment
through the Cosmic Christ who is all and in all,
when we encounter other religions
and philosophies [Ephesians, Colossians].
Invite us in the spirit of hope
through the Coming Christ
as we counter hopelessness [1 Thessalonians]
or overconfidence [2 Thessalonians].
Install in us the spirit of courage
to transform heresy, chaotic structure,
and confused morality
within the church and in society
[1, 2 Timothy, Titus].
Install in us the spirit of love
to resolve overt and covert domination
in interpersonal and systemic forms [Philemon].

Instruct us, Spirit of Truth, what it means to be:
a worshipping community on the move
that finds Sabbath-rest in flux,
as we, the resident alien, fix our eyes on Jesus
and the heavenly city [Hebrews],
a learning community of wisdom that leads us
to perfection and freedom,
as we befriend you, the source of all the perfect
and good gifts [James],
an exilic community that embodies the eternal hope
of you, the Living God,
for we are precious in your sight, peculiar
to the world [1 Peter],

a discerning community that can tell truth
from deceptions,
and live in honor rather than shame [2 Peter, Jude],
a koinonia-community that loves one another
in the purity of heart and mutual forgiveness
[1–3 John],
a witnessing community through worship envisions
God's judgment and victory over evil and chaos
because the Lamb defines the end of history
[Revelation].

BLESSING

May God who is able, faithful, holy, and loving give us
the will to do these things,
give us the grace to be and to do God's will
that the work begun in us may be brought
to wholeness. Amen!

CLOSING PRAYER

Gracious God,
give to these your children and your friends
the grace and power we need to serve you,
make us faithful pastors, merciful priests, bold prophets,
wise teachers, patient counselors,
spiritual administrators.
For the sake of Christ's love that compels us,
we offer ourselves as living sacrifices to you;
through Christ our Lord,
in the unity and mystery of the Holy Spirit,
one God, now and for ever. Amen!

BENEDICTION

Go in peace
to love and serve God, and your neighbor,
in all that you do,
and the God of shalom be with you always!
Amen!

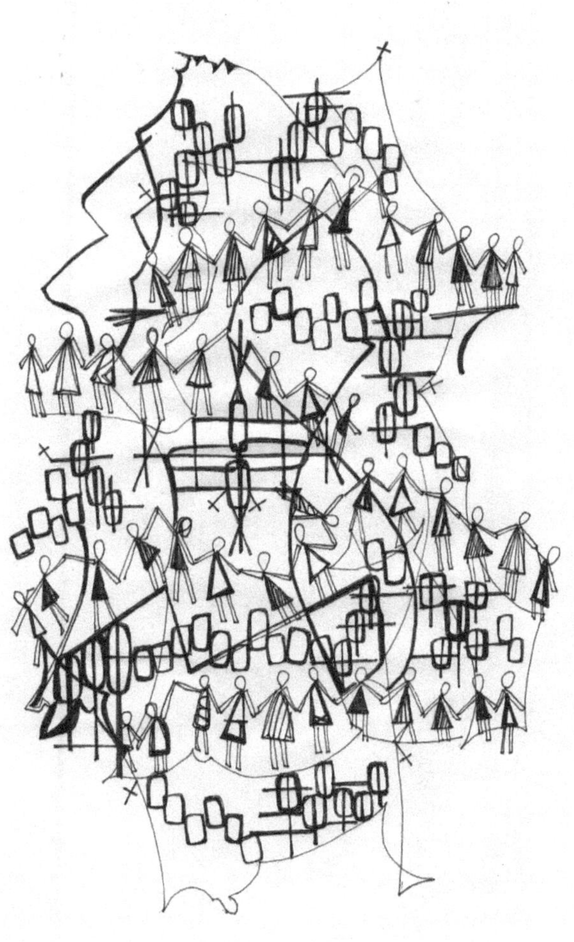

The church in worship and service

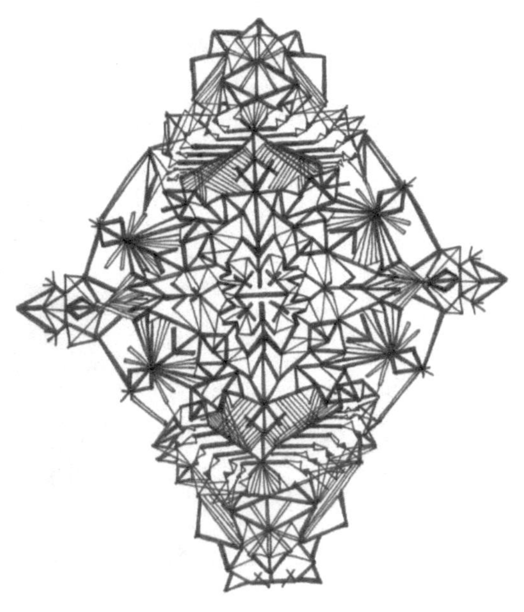

Persecuted Cross, kaleidoscopic faith

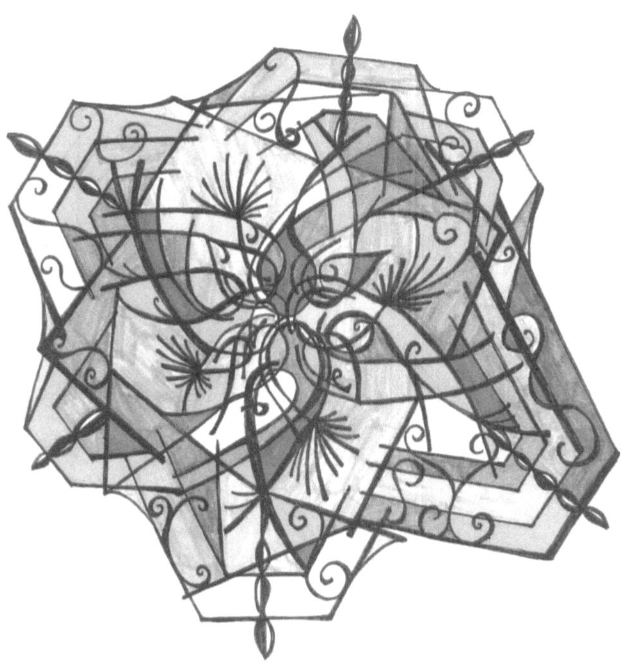

Powerful witness

Bibliography

Begbie, Jeremy. *Beholding the Glory: Incarnation through the Arts*. Grand Rapids: Baker, 2003.

Benson, Bruce. *The Phenomenology of Prayer*. Bronx: Fordham University Press, 2005.

Bonhoeffer, Dietrich. *Psalms: The Prayer Book of the Bible*. Translated by Isabel Mary. Oxford: SLG, 1982.

Brown, Frank Burch. *Good Taste, Bad Taste, and Christian Taste: Aesthetics in Religious Life*. New York: Oxford University Press, 2000.

Brueggemann, Walter. *Awed to Heaven, Rooted in Earth: Prayers of Walter Brueggemann*. Minneapolis: Fortress, 2003.

Cullmann, Oscar. *Prayer in the New Testament*. Translated by John Bowden. Overtures to Biblical Theology. Minneapolis: Fortress, 1995.

Debray, Regis. *The New Testament: Through 100 Masterpieces of Art*. Translated, adapted, and augmented by Benjamin Lifson. London: Merrell, 2004.

Drury, John. *Painting the Word: Christian Pictures and Their Meanings*. New Haven: Yale University Press, 1999.

Duck, Ruth C. *Finding Words for Worship: A Guide for Leaders*. Louisville: Westminster John Knox, 1995.

Longenecker, Richard N. *Into God's Presence: Prayer in the New Testament*. Grand Rapids: Eerdmans, 2001.

Nouwen, Henri J. M. *Behold the Beauty of the Lord: Praying with Icons*. Notre Dame: Ave Maria, 2007.

Roberts, Elizabeth. *Earth Prayers from around the World: 365 Prayers, Poems, and Invocations for Honoring the Earth*. New York: HarperCollins, 1991.

Roberts, Helene, and Rachel Hall. *Iconographic Index to New Testament Subjects Represented in Photographs and Slides of Paintings in the Visual Collections, Fine Arts Library, Harvard University*. 2 vols.

Garland Reference Library of the Humanities 1154. New York: Garland, 1992, 2001.

Stookey, Laurence Hull. *Let the Whole Church Say Amen! A Guide for Those Who Pray in Public*. Nashville: Abingdon, 2001.

Viladesau, Richard. *Theology and the Arts: Encountering God through Music, Art, and Rhetoric*. New York: Paulist, 2000.

Yancey, Philip. *Prayer: Does It Make Any Difference?* Grand Rapids: Zondervan, 2006.

www.ingramcontent.com/pod-product-compliance
Lightning Source LLC
LaVergne TN
LVHW051007080826
845145LV00009B/2506

9781606087947